HOW TO BE A LITERARY AGENT

An Introductory Guide to Literary Representation

RICHARD MARIOTTI
&
BRUCE FIFE

PICCADILLY BOOKS
COLORADO SPRINGS, CO

Cover design by John Reinhardt

Piccadilly Books
P.O. Box 25203
Colorado Springs, CO 80936

International sales and inquires contact:
 EPS
 20 Park Drive
 Romford Essex RM1 4LH, UK
or
 EPS
 P.O. Box 1344
 Studio City, CA 91614, USA

Library of Congress Cataloging-in-Publication Data

Fife, Bruce, 1952
    How to be a literary agent: an introductory guide to literary
 representation/ by Richard Mariotti and Bruce Fife.
        p.   cm.
    Includes bibliographical references and index.
    ISBN 0-941599-26-4
    1. Literary agents--United States. I. Title.
 PN163.F54 1994
 070.5'2--dc20   94-15179

Simultaneously published in Australia, UK, and USA
Printed in Canada

CONTENTS

Chapter 1

INTRODUCTION

If you took a survey, you would find that most people have inner desires to become published authors and see their names in print. People from all walks of life are actively pursuing this dream. The vast majority of these people are not trained writers, but average people working everyday jobs. They have a compelling desire to entertain others with their stories or to share their knowledge. The thrill and excitement of possibly receiving praise, honor, and huge royalties is fueled by the success stories of many first-time authors who have actually achieved this dream. Getting published, however, is not an easy task. Most budding authors never get their works published, let alone become rich and famous.

Book publishers are deluged with unsolicited manuscripts from first-time authors. Although publishers are continually looking for new authors with salable books, they receive far more submissions than they can adequately evaluate. The vast majority of these submissions, for various reasons, are never published. Editors do not have the time to read every manuscript that crosses their desks. Literary agents provide a valuable service to publishers by weeding out unpublishable material and delivering only works that would be of interest to publishers. For this reason, most all of the large publishing companies and many of the medium and smaller-sized companies refuse even to look at unsolicited or unagented manuscripts. More and more publishing companies are adopting this policy, making it extremely difficult for authors to approach publishers directly.

Because many publishers refuse to look at manuscripts sent to them directly by authors, a great demand exists for literary agents. Even if a work has been accepted for publication without an agent's help, many publishers recommend that the author get an agent before closing the deal. These publishers prefer to work with knowledgeable agents rather than with inexperienced authors.

Every year, hundreds of thousands of authors seek to get published. Because many publishers refuse to consider unagented or unsolicited works, new authors feel they are forced to find agents if they are to accomplish their goal. Unlike other service businesses, literary agents don't have to spend time seeking new clients. Potential clients seek them. Agents are looked on as having a special magic which allows them to sell manuscripts quickly at the highest price possible. Although this is not a realistic expectation, it encourages writers to search for agents to represent them. Most businesses spend a great deal of time and money in advertising and promotion in an effort to attract new customers or clients. Literary agents spend very little, if anything at all.

Established agents are flooded with manuscript submissions and, as a result, they become very selective and work only with authors who have already had several works published. Some agents receive so many inquiries that they have unlisted business phones or delete their address listings in trade directories. Many will take a new client only if the author is recommended by one of the agent's current clients or a respected business associate.

Some agents are employed by literary agencies and work as part of a team; however, most agents are self-employed and work out of home-based offices. You will find successful literary agents who are college graduates and even have law degrees, while others have no more than a high school education. There are no qualifications, training, or licensing requirements necessary to work as a literary agent. Although some agencies hire people right out of college, most agents receive their training as former book editors, publishers' sales reps, or from being published authors themselves.

While there are advantages to working in cities with large publishing industries, it is not necessary. A literary agent can live and work anywhere in the country. All work can be conducted on the phone and through the mail. An agent in Texas can sell a manuscript from an author in Oregon to a publisher in New York almost as easily as if all three were located in the same city. For this reason, self-employed agents can live almost anywhere and still operate a successful business.

The cost to set up your own literary agency is minimal, particularly if you work out of your home. For established agencies, advertising is generally unnecessary. Since literary representation is a service business, there is no inventory to buy and keep track of. If you already own a word processor or computer, you need only buy stationery and envelopes.

Success will not come overnight. As with any business, it will take time and effort to make literary representation a profitable venture. Your success will depend largely on the amount of time and effort you invest. If you are serious about becoming a literary agent, you can be a success.

If you like to read books, literary representation can be a fun and rewarding career. Start-up costs are minimal, formal training is not required, and you can work out of the comfort of your own home. With the increasing demand from the publishing industry for authors to get literary representation, the need for competent agents will continue to grow. For many people, literary representation provides an ideal career opportunity.

The primary purpose of this book is to serve as an introduction to the profession of literary representation. It presents the basic information all literary agents are expected to know. It cannot contain every single aspect or detail about literary representation; much of what an agent learns comes through experience. Readers sincerely interested in becoming literary agents should strive to learn everything they can about the publishing industry. Ideally, they should gain first-hand experience working under the tutelage of an established agent. Experience can also be obtained by working in a publishing company. A third way to gain practical experience is to be your own agent and become a published author. Many successful agents started out as writers and gained the experience they needed by marketing their own works.

Another purpose of this book is to show writers how to be their own agents and get their works published. Writers don't need to work with agents if they know how to approach publishers, properly prepare and send submissions, and negotiate a publishing contract—all of which is covered in this book. You will learn how to present yourself like a professional writer and get the same respect given to successful authors. You will also learn about publishing agreements and how to negotiate the best possible terms.

Whether you're interested in becoming a literary agent or simply want to learn the inside secrets of getting published, this book will show you how.

Chapter 2

LITERARY REPRESENTATION

George Bernau, a 42-year-old, semi-retired motion picture lawyer from California, dreamed of being a writer. Although he had never had a word published, he began writing his first novel, *Promises to Keep*. This book grew out of his fascination with the Kennedy assassination. It poses several questions. What if John F. Kennedy was shot but not killed in November 1963? What might have happened during a second Kennedy term? Although the names were changed and fictional characters used, Bernau's huge 1,400-page manuscript was based on this premise.

Bernau worked on the novel for nearly a decade before he sent it to the Scott Meredith Literary Agency, one of the country's largest and most successful agencies. The agency was amazed at Bernau's extensive research and his ability to develop the novel into a "real page-turner."

Feeling they had a winner on their hands, they decided to put it up for auction. They sent the manuscript to 13 publishers, setting the closing date for the auction two weeks later. Immediately after the first weekend, publishers started offering various amounts, all around the $250,000 level. These offers were turned down because it was still too far in advance of the closing date and they knew some publishers would not have had the chance to finish reading the manuscript. More offers came in, but Warner Books' stunning floor bid of $750,000 knocked them all out of contention.

An editor at another publishing house that offered $500,000 said their bid was based on figures hypothesizing a net sale of 75,000-100,000 hardcover copies at $19.95, with a 15 percent author's royalty, estimated subsidiary rights income of $185,000 in foreign sales, and a $35,000 book club sale. For the paperback edition, the publisher estimated net sales of 750,000-1,000,000 copies at a 10 percent royalty. If these figures seem low, the editor said, for a novel with "the intrinsic interest" of *Promises to Keep,* "it's because this is a first-time author who is completely unknown and our calculations must be based on our lowest estimate of proceeds from all sales categories."

At the time, Warner's advance was a record for a first novel. Another author, Sally Beauman's first mainstream novel, *Destiny,* went to Bantam for $1.15 million. She wasn't really a first-time author since she had some romance novels published before that. As authors build a name for themselves, their works become more marketable and advances increase. Judith Krantz received a $2.2 million advance for her book, *Mistral's Daughter.* James Clavell received $5 million for *Whirlwind.* Gail Sheehy received $1 million for *Pathfinders.* Random House paid Norman Mailer $5 million on a four-novel deal. Marion Zimmer Bradley received $3.5 million for two novels. Arthur C. Clarke received $4 million for three novels. Actor Burt Reynolds received $1 million for his autobiography. Although Burt Reynolds is not a famous author, his status as a celebrity influenced publishers' offers.

Most books don't come anywhere near the figures these authors received, but the potential is there. A good agent with a good book can make a big profit. How do agents find authors with big books and how do they approach and sell these books at the best possible prices? This book will give you the clues to the answers to these questions.

In this chapter, you will learn how publishing companies and literary agents operate and interact with each other. You will be taken through the process of how books are submitted, evaluated, sold, and published. This will give you a broad overview of the publishing process and how literary agents fit in.

HOW LITERARY REPRESENTATION WORKS

Working with New Clients

Literary agents are basically brokers. They bring buyers (publishers) and sellers (writers) together. Literary agents seek out suitable publishers and negotiate contracts on the author's behalf. In compensation for the agent's efforts, authors share with their agents the profits derived from the sale of the manuscripts.

Most agents concentrate on book-length manuscripts only. The money for short stories, poetry, and magazine articles is usually too small for them to bother with. A few do handle articles and other short pieces, but only for successful clients or well-known authors seeking publication in the largest and highest-paying magazines.

Literary agents spend a great deal of their time reading— searching for salable manuscripts. All agents actively seek talented new writers—even established agencies with large clienteles. Successful agents are busy people, dividing their time between various projects all at different stages of development. Their time isdevoted to evaluating new submissions, reading manuscripts, preparing and sending submissions, negotiating contracts, and answering authors' questions. Most of their time, however, is spent evaluating new material from both current and potential clients.

Because many publishers refuse to consider unagented authors and because agents know the publishing business and can sell a manuscript when an unagented author can't, writers are constantly seeking agents to represent them. Consequently, agents are flooded with an endless stream of query letters and unsolicited manuscripts from writers. They receive so much material that many agents discourage submissions, considering new clients only if they are recommended by a current client or publisher.

The accepted way for an author to establish contact with an agent is by sending a query letter along with a self-addressed, stamped, return envelope (SASE). The query letter briefly describes the manuscript, gives the author's credentials or qualifications, and requests permission to send the manuscript. If the author's idea or story shows promise, the agent will invite him or her to send a book proposal or the complete manuscript.

If the author has written a nonfiction book, he may also send a book proposal along with the query letter. If it is a novel, the author should include a detailed synopsis with the letter. The agent can then request sample chapters or the complete manuscript. Many first-time authors, unfamiliar with submission procedures, send agents unsolicited manuscripts without bothering with a query letter or book proposal. If the author includes a SASE with the submission, the agent can send a response. Because agents receive so many submissions they cannot afford to respond unless a SASE is included. Unless they are interested in the author's material, some agents will not send a response even if they receive a SASE. Of course, agents will respond to any submission they like, regardless of whether a SASE was included or not.

Agents receive a variety of material from both published and unpublished writers of all skill levels and from all walks of life. Searching through these materials can be fascinating. Some manuscripts are so bad they're comical, while others are written with spellbinding imagination and clarity. Agents don't need to, and can't afford to, spend time reading everything that is sent to them. Most of the material can be eliminated for one reason or another with just a brief examination. Material that appears to have promise will receive careful consideration.

Agents usually specialize in certain types of books, such

as novels, screenplays, how-to, or self-help. Some may be open to a wider range of subjects and handle any adult fiction and nonfiction, or they may focus on just a few specific subjects, such as science fiction and fantasy. Agencies that handle a wide variety of subjects usually employ agents who specialize. This allows each agent to be more effective. They learn the needs of publishers in their particular area of specialization and make personal contacts with the in-house editors. This close, personal contact helps keep agents in tune with publishers' needs and wants.

When an agent finds a manuscript he feels he can sell, he accepts the writer as a client. The author is sent a contract or letter of agreement specifying the agent's commission, fees, and other terms. Once that is signed, the agent works with the writer to polish the manuscript to maximize its chances of selling. The agent helps the author prepare suitable submission materials and then sends them to select publishers, offering the manuscript for sale.

Marketing Manuscripts

The agent does not send material to just any publisher, but chooses the most appropriate for the manuscript. Although a publishing house may produce many different types of books, each editor within the company may handle only certain types of books. Often, large publishing companies have imprints (subsidiary companies) that specialize in certain types of books. Some editors work only with science fiction, others with romance or cookbooks. A western novel, sent to an editor who deals only wlith how-to books, would reject the submission. Agents know this and direct their clients' works to appropriate editors.

Writers often do not understand how properly to prepare and send submissions. A frequent problem is sending material to an editor who has no interest in the book's subject. Also, a great deal of material sent to publishers is not written well enough for publication. Agents screen manuscripts and eliminate those that are unpublishable. They send editors only material that would be of interest to them. Publishers assume that material submitted by agents is more likely to fit their needs than the random submissions they receive directly from authors. For these reasons, materials submitted by agents are given far more attention than those that are not.

Even though agents market only works they believe are publishable, no agent is successful at selling every manuscript he represents. Some Pulitzer prize-winning and bestselling books have been rejected dozens of times before finding an interested publisher. So even some of the best books may be hard to sell. Some manuscripts, particularly novels, are offered to many publishers before they are purchased. Even though an agent may market a publishable work, he still may not find an interested publisher. Economic conditions, competition with other works, and current trends all play a part in what types of books will sell. A good book that might easily have sold last year may be impossible to sell this year. Agents who keep abreast of the trends in the book industry and know what types of books are currently selling are the most successful.

Publishing Houses

An agent's contact with publishing companies is with the editorial staff. There are several different types of editors and their titles and functions vary from house to house. The top executive at a publishing house is the publisher. Under him, the editorial positions in order are: the editor-in-chief, editorial director, executive editor, senior editor, editor, associate editor, assistant editor, and editorial assistant. This is the basic editorial hierarchy in large publishing houses. Not all houses have all these positions, and some use different titles (e.g., managing editor, acquisitions editor, etc.).

The top management concern themselves primarily with administrative duties. Submissions sent to them from authors or unknown agents are passed unread to the editorial staff. The higher management deal directly with literary agents with whom they have a long relationship and who represent top name writers. The core of the acquisition process is handled by senior editors and editors. Associate editors and assistant editors may be allowed to acquire books, although they may still be assigned most of their projects by higher-ups. They are often the best ones to whom to send submissions. They don't have as many agent contacts as the more established editors and are anxious to find promising new books and agents to help boost their careers. At the tail end of the editorial ladder is the editorial assistant. This is an entry-level position. These people are assigned to assist other editors by answering their phones, typing correspondence, etc. They usually can't acquire books, but may bring promising books to an editor's attention. Frequently, editoral assistants are called first readers because they screen new manuscripts before passing them on to other editors. They are the ones who are usually assigned the task of reviewing unsolicited submissions.

Acquiring new books is only one part of an editor's job. Not only do they review new submissions, but they must continually work on projects that have already been acquired and are in various stages of the editorial/production process. Besides evaluating new submissions, they may also be negotiating contracts, editing manuscripts, proofreading galleys, and writing copy for the back cover of books, while still handling various other day-to-day responsibilities. Most of an editor's time is taken up preparing for and attending meetings, discussing marketing and promotional aspects of various projects, meeting and talking with agents, dealing with problems, and answering questions. These activities eat up so much time, editors typically spend many hours editing and reviewing new submissions at home after normal work hours.

Some publishing houses have editors whose primary job is to acquire new books. After a publishing agreement has been signed with the agent or author, the project is passed on to a project editor or a line editor, who handles the editorial work. Editors at most houses, however, edit the projects they acquire.

Although authors themselves send in the largest quantity of submissions, comparatively few are chosen for publication. The greatest number of submissions accepted for publication are sent in by agents. This is particularly true for large publishing houses. Editors and agents often work closely together, meet to discuss new projects, and even have lunch together. Material submitted by agents has a much better chance of being published. Not only do agents represent most of the big-name authors and celebrities, but they provide a valuable service for the editors by screening manuscripts. When an editor receives a manuscript from an agent, he knows the agent has read it, liked it, and believes it to be commercially publishable. If the agent has a good relationship with the editor and has given him good books in the past, then the editor will be anxious to review material the agent recommends. The reverse is also true: if the editor has been dissatisfied with previous submissions from an agent, new submissions will receive little attention.

A large publishing house may receive hundreds of unsolicited manuscripts a week. This material is called "slush" and is set aside in what is referred to as the "slush pile". Some publishers will return unsolicited manuscripts unopened; others may open them but only to insert a rejection notice before being returned. Those companies that look at unsolicited submissions assign busy editorial assistants to sort through the slush. The slush pile is given such low priority that material may sit for weeks before being evaluated. Because it is unlikely that editors will find something publishable in the slush pile, they don't spend much time with it. Most of these submissions are rejected after reading only a few pages. Editors are often prejudiced against unpublished authors and will inadvertently reject good material. This is what happened to Tom Clancy's first novel, *The Hunt for Red October*. Every large publishing house he submitted it to rejected it. Eventually, it was published by a small publisher and became a national bestseller.

Unsolicited query letters and proposals receive similar treatment. However, it is more likely that an editor will read a one-page query letter than a 300-page manuscript. So, queries and proposals are read first. Because of the large number of submissions, most publishers prefer to receive query letters or proposals as their first contact instead of complete manuscripts.

Sometimes editors will generate their own ideas for books. They can see the trends in publishing. They know what types of books are selling and what topics are hot. Instead of just sitting back and hoping for the right manuscript to arrive, they are encouraged to contact writers and agents with their ideas. Agents can suggest writers capable of taking on such assignments. If an editor has a good relationship with an agent, the editor might call him when looking for a writer. This provides the agent an almost sure sale if the writer he chooses can handle the job. Even though the editor initiates the project, he may still reject the agent's manuscript if it doesn't meet his expectations.

Most rejected submissions are returned with a form rejection letter. If the editor liked the material, but still had to turn it down, he may write a personal rejection letter. Sometimes, he may even offer suggestions or invite the author to submit a revised manuscript or new material in the future. If the work was submitted by an agent that the editor knows, out of courtesy he will usually send a personal letter whether she liked the book or not.

Just because the first reader may have liked a book does not mean it will be published. If the editor likes the book, the manuscript has passed only the first of many steps toward publication. It still has to be passed on to other editors for continued evaluation.

Usually junior editors must pass worthwhile projects up to more senior editors who, after approval, will present them to management. Although each editor has the power to reject a book, only the publisher or editor-in-chief has the power to approve it for publication.

In an editorial meeting, the management and staff meet together to discuss new books. Each of the editors presents the books he wants to buy. In the presentation, the editors describe the book, tell why they like it, why they should publish it, who will buy it, and why it is going to make money. Everyone present has the opportunity to ask questions or state objections to the proposed projects. The publisher or whoever is presiding over the meeting makes the final decision on whether or not to buy the book.

Not every book presented in the editorial meeting is bought—most aren't. Out of dozens of projects presented, only a handful are approved for publication. In a meeting, an editor may have only one of several projects accepted.

Making the Sale

When a publishing house accepts a book for publication, it is sent to the production department to determine how much it will cost to produce. The production cost is used to determine the retail price. From this, the author's advance (royalties paid before the book is published) is calculated. Typically, the advance is equal to the royalty the book will make in its first printing. First printings for most books (particularly hardcover) are modest and generally do not exceed 10,000 copies. This is often the estimated amount the publisher expects to sell in one year. Larger first-print runs are reserved for books written by big-name authors and celebrities, in anticipation of becoming bestsellers. The advance is figured by taking the number of books in the first printing and multiplying it by the retail price and by the royalty rate. For example, a trade paperback book with a first printing of 10,000 copies and a retail price of $9.95 at six percent royalty (a standard trade paperback royalty) will give you a total of $5,970. Rounded up to $6,000, this is the maximum advance the publisher would offer.

With this figure, the editor will call the author or agent with an offer detailing the rights to be purchased, the amount of the advance, and the royalty rate. This is when negotiations start. The agent acts on the author's behalf to hammer out terms of the contract.

The editor, anticipating that the agent will request a larger advance, will typically offer an amount under the maximum limit. This allows room for negotiation. The agent will usually suggest a larger advance. The editor may counter, but once he has reached his authorized limit, that is it. He cannot go higher. The actual negotiation process may take several days, as the agent may want to contact the author at each stage of the game to get his approval before finalizing the terms. Most publishing contracts are very similar. Other than the amount of the advance, the contract that is given to a first-time author will be pretty much the same as the one given to an established author. Agents know what terms are negotiable and how far to push. Although agents don't need to be lawyers, they do need to understand the details of publishing agreements and know what terms could be modified in their client's favor. Unless the manuscript is extraordinary, if the agent is representing a new author, he has little bargaining power. A successful author with several bestsellers will give the agent a much stronger negotiating position. The most important terms that are usually negotiated are the size of the advance, royalties, and control of subsidiary rights. As long as the book remains in print or licensing opportunities exist, the agent acts as the author's representative and receives a share of the profits.

Most publishers are primarily interested in purchasing the publishing rights to the manuscripts they buy. The agent can negotiate to retain most of the subsidiary rights so that he may sell these rights to others. These include such things as serial rights, dramatic and movie rights, audio and video rights, and foreign rights. Often, publishers do not put much effort into selling subsidiary rights. An aggressive agent can have more success selling these rights, benefitting both the agent and author.

Publication

Once the terms are agreed to, a publishing contract is drawn up and signed. A deadline for the completion and delivery of the manuscript is stated in the agreement (most books by published authors are sold before they are completed). The book is assigned a publication date based on this deadline.

When the editor receives the completed manuscript, he does a gross edit, which includes any recommendation for restructuring or rewriting he feels is necessary, and returns the manuscript to the author for reworking. After the author returns the manuscript, the editor does a line edit, going over the work line-by-line, checking for style, grammar, punctuation, and consistency. Again the manuscript is returned to the author for approval. The manuscript is then copy-edited and further refined. The manuscript is typeset in book format and galleys or page proofs are made. A copy of the proofs is sent to the author for one final check, primarily for typographical errors. This is the last stage at which changes can be made. During this time the dust-jact is designed and cover copy written. The book is then published and advance copies sent to the author or agent. Although the books have been published, the official publication date will still be several weeks away. This allows the publisher time to announce the book, take prepublication orders, and send books to bookstores so that the stores have them in stock on the publication date.

The publisher's publicity department then contacts the author for possible book signings, radio and television interviews, and other publicity appearances.

SCRIPT AGENTS

A literary agent who specializes in selling scripts is called a *script* or *dramatic agent.* Script agents sell stage and screenplays to theatrical and film production companies as well as to publishers. Many agents function as both literary and script agents, but most choose to specialize in either one or the other.

Script agents approach publishing companies in much the same way literary agents approach publishers. They contact publishers who produce scripts and screenplays, as well as theatrical, television, and movie studios or production companies.

Although many of the large publishing companies refuse to accept submissions from unagented authors, most publishers will at least take a look at anything sent to them. This is not true with production companies. It is nearly impossible for a writer to approach a production company without the aid of an agent. Some of the smaller companies may consider material from an unagented author who presents himself in a professional manner, but only rarely. A writer who wants to sell to theater and film studios needs to work with an agent. Consequently, qualified script agents are in demand.

Production companies, like publishers, are bombarded with submissions, the vast majority of which will never be produced. Unlike book publishers, however, production companies are also plagued by "nuisance" lawsuits. These lawsuits come primarily from inexperienced or unagented authors who claim their scripts have been stolen. A writer may send in a script for use on a popular television show and later claim that the show used portions of his script. For example, his plot may have dealt with drug dealers kidnapping the mayor's daughter and holding her for ransom. The television show may air a show where drug dealers kidnap the district attorney's daughter. The writer will then claim the show stole his script. Despite some similarity in the two plots, the company did not steal the script. In fact, considering the thousands of scripts submitted to each show, using the same characters and basic theme, it would be impossible to produce new episodes week after week without touching on themes found in many submissions. Because of these nuisance lawsuits, production companies do not normally read unagented submissions.

Production companies could still be troubled by lawsuits from agented authors, but agents weed out the amateurs who cause most of the trouble. Agents will also have authors sign a release form that is submitted with the manuscript. The release form acknowledges that the production company has access to literary materials and ideas which may be similar to the author's and that the company will not be held liable for compensation to the author because of the use of similar material. Agents can get release forms from the production companies.

To be successful, script agents must keep up-to-date with what is happening in the entertainment industry. *Daily Variety* and *The Hollywood Reporter* are the two major daily business papers of the entertainment industry. Another publication of interest is *The Hollywood Scriptwriter,* which is a newsletter aimed at new and professional scriptwriters. It includes agency updates along with an Annual Agency Issue every summer.

The process of selling a script and negotiating the terms of the contract are somewhat more complex than that of a book. It takes most good script agents many years of experience to acquire the skills and knowledge to be effective. For this reason, it is best for literary agents to work with script agents when trying to sell production rights. The script agent would function as a subagent for the literary agent and be entitled to share in the commission. When agents use subagents, commissions increase by 5-10 percent to compensate for the efforts of both agents. For further information about scripts and the film industry, see the Appendix.

BUILDING A CAREER

Every author and agent dreams of making the big deal and selling a book with an advance of six figures. When reading the trade magazines or newspapers, you will come across stories of authors who have sold their latest works and received six-figure advances. Unfortunately, huge advances are relatively rare and only a few of the largest publishing conglomerates can afford to pay these sums. Most advances, even from the large companies, are less than $10,000. Advances for first-time authors are frequently less than $5,000. Books by first-time authors are a high risk, so publishers are conservative with print runs and advances.

There are exceptions and there have been several notable works from first-time authors in recent years. Amy Tan's bestselling *The Joy Luck Club* brought a $50,000 advance and was made into a major motion picture. Other novels from first-time authors that have earned advances of $100,000 or more or became blockbuster bestsellers include: Judith Guest's *Ordinary People*, Naomi Ragen's *Jephte's Daughters*, Bryce Courtenay's *The Power of One*, John Lucas's *Tables,* Judith

Merkle Riley's *A Vision of Light*, Scott Turow's *Presumed Innocent*, and Michael Chabon's *Mysteries of Pittsburgh.*

Fueled by the success of these and other first-time novelists, unpublished writers dream of huge advances and bestseller status. For the great majority of new writers, their hopes will remain only a dream. Most published novelists become successful very gradually. Their early works often remain unpublished. They build an audience and a career slowly, receiving big money only after having several books published.

Big deals for new authors are extremely rare. Most of the big advances you hear about are reserved for proven writers with long track records and huge audiences of loyal readers.

Most new agents must start out by representing relatively new authors. The odds of finding an unpublished genius and making a six-figure deal are so remote, it is not worth thinking about. Instead, concentrate on smaller deals and take it one step at a time. The bigger deals will come later, as you and your authors gain experience and recognition. Striving for the big deal and not accomplishing it will only lead to discouragement. Concentrate on developing a career, rather than looking for the one-shot bonanza.

Finding talented authors to work with is just one ingredient in developing a successful career as an agent. Another ingredient is treating your clients with respect. Think of them as business partners. You must be sincerely interested in helping your clients build their writing careers. As they achieve publishing success, your business will grow. Use your talents and skills to help your clients in any way you can. Help prepare their works so they have the greatest chance of selling and do all you can to market them successfully. You won't be able to sell every manuscript you market, but you should give each one your best effort.

Authors can often sense an agent who lacks enthusiasm or motivation. Relations with these agents are quickly terminated. Authors are naturally curious about the agent's marketing progress. If the author does not receive any communication from the agent, he will not know if the agent is really putting forth a sincere effort to sell the work. The agent should periodically give authors progress reports. These reports should include a list of publishers contacted and copies of publishers' responses. You might even send copies of rejection letters. Giving this information to the author lets him know you are diligently working to sell his work. If making a sale is slow or even nonexistent, at least the author will not accuse you of being lazy or dishonest. You've shown him the results of your efforts.

Editorial help is one of the most valuable services an agent can offer a new writer. Reworking a manuscript to improve it will enhance its chances of selling and help the author become a better writer. The agent does not have to be a literary critic or a skilled copyeditor, as he can have freelancers perform these services.

Some agents and writers have expressed opinions that agents should only be involved in selling manuscripts and negotiating contracts, and look down on agents who provide editorial and other services. They reason that a successful agent should make all of his money from selling manuscripts. This way, he would have a greater interest in making the sale. Although there is some merit in this idea, many new writers need a little extra help and appreciate these services. An agency that has been in business for many years has close personal contacts with publishing professionals, and many big-name agents can afford to turn away unpublished writers. But newer agencies have to establish a clientele of successful authors, and those are usually developed from less experienced writers. New agents must take chances by working with new authors. Agents who provide critiquing, copyediting, proofreading, and publicity services will enhance the author's chances for success. An agent who can provide these extra services to a new author is an added benefit.

Of course, writers need to be cautious of agents who focus their attention on selling services rather than selling manuscripts. Some less successful agents depend on these services as their primary source of income.

Since the author is entering into a business relationship with an agent, he has the right to ask for references or other information. Be prepared to provide potential clients with lists of satisfied clients and recently-sold books.

In the early stages of representation, you won't have many references. Your background and experience will be your biggest selling points. Obviously, first-hand experience working for a literary agency or publishing company will give you the best preparation for this business. If you don't have practical work experience, the next best thing is to have experience as a published author—being your own literary agent by selling your own works. If you have been successful selling your own books, you demonstrate that you know something about the publishing industry and that you are an accomplished writer. Anyone who can sell his own works is looked on with awe and envy by novice writers who have tried in vain to become published themselves. They will assume you know the elusive secrets of getting published.

In order to work as a literary agent without the experience of working in the publishing industry, you must at least have experience selling your own works. Another way to gain practical experience is to volunteer your services to other writers. If you study this book and increase your knowledge of the publishing industry by reading writer's magazines and books, you could offer to help other writers prepare and submit their works. This way, you can build up a list of references and gain the respect of prospective clients. You might offer to help sell an author's first book with the stipulation that, if you are successful, he will pay you a commission for marketing future books. You may offer your initial services for free, but the client should expect to pay expenses such as photocopying, postage, and stationery, which he would incur anyway.

Any agent who sets up a business without first gaining proper knowledge and experience is doing his clients a disservice. Editors can spot a submission from an inexperienced agent just as easily as they can an unpublished author. Both make the same mistakes. Submissions from such agents are thrown into the slush pile and given the same respect unsolicited material receives. The chances of making a sale under such conditions are remote.

Study this book, study other books on getting published, read writer's magazines, and gain first-hand experience. Two books I highly recommend reading are *The Awful Truth About Publishing: Why They Always Reject Your Manuscript and What You Can Do About It* by John Boswell and *How to Be Your Own Literary Agent* by Richard Curtis. Both of these books were written by successful literary agents and contain valuable inside information about the process of getting published and working with editors. There are many other useful books on preparing and submitting manuscripts and negotiating contracts (see the Appendix for details). Commit yourself to learning all you can about the publishing industry, keep up your enthusiasm, and put your best effort into every manuscript you market. If you do this, you will be on the road to success.

Chapter 3

ESTABLISHING YOUR BUSINESS

In this chapter, you will learn how to set up your own literary agency. You will be introduced to the legal and tax aspects of starting and operating a service business, as well as gain helpful insights into working in an at-home office.

TYPE OF BUSINESS

One of the first decisions you must make when you start a business is to determine which of the three basic types of business entities to use—sole proprietorship, partnership, or corporation. There are legal and tax considerations that enter into this decision.

A sole proprietorship is the simplest form of business organization and the easiest to operate, especially if you work out of your home. With a sole proprietorship, you *are* the business. You have total control and responsibility of how the company is financed and how it functions. All profits the company makes are yours, but so are the losses. You are also personally responsible for all of the company's debts and liabilities, which means that if your company cannot pay an obligation, the creditor can go after your personal assets to satisfy this debt. When you figure your taxable income for the year, you must add any profit, or subtract any loss, you have from your business. This is reported on a form Schedule C, *Profit or Loss From Business*, and included with your tax return Form 1040. Most businesses are sole proprietorships.

A partnership is a relationship between two or more persons who join together to carry on a trade or business. Each person contributes money, property, labor, or skill, and expects to share in the profits and losses of the business. Many small businesses can increase their assets, have access to useful equipment, and pool the skills and talents of two or more individuals in a partnership that can make the business more successful. Partnerships must file their taxes on Form 1065, *U.S. Partnership Return of Income*. This requires more time and energy to prepare than the form for the sole proprietor. A joint undertaking to share expenses or the mere co-ownership of property that is used in the business is not a partnership. A spouse or children, for example, who help out in the business are not necessarily partners even though they may be compensated for their labors. A partnership can be formed with a verbal agreement, however, it is best to have a formal signed contract. This document specifies what has been invested by each partner and exactly what is expected from them and by them.

Corporations are normally owned by a group of people who are called shareholders. The shareholders run the company through a board of directors. Officers and employees of the corporation may also be shareholders or members of the board of directors. Corporations are entitled to special tax deductions not available to sole proprietors or partnerships, but because they are considered separate entities from their owners, the corporate profits are taxed. Because of this, owners of small corporations could end up paying more taxes than sole proprietors or partnerships. One of the primary advantages of using a corporation is that shareholders cannot be held responsible for the company's debts and liabilities. This gives owners some degree of protection not given to other types of businesses. If the business goes bankrupt, it is not reflected in the owner's credit report. Also, legal judgments against the corporation are limited to the business, and lawyers usually cannot go after individual shareholders to satisfy debts. A major disadvantage is that corporations are more closely regulated by the government, and the paperwork for starting and maintaining this type of business is an unnecessary burden to many new small businesses.

A special type of corporation designed primarily for smaller businesses is an *S corporation*. This type of corporation allows small businesses to benefit from many of the advantages of being incorporated—including protection from liability—without over-burdening them with regulations and paperwork. Since this entity was designed for small businesses, the government has put a limit on the maximum number of shareholders or owners an S corporation can have. In many states it is possible for a husband and wife team to satisfy requirements and form an S corporation. However, the amount of work required and expense of setting up and maintaining the business, which includes many bothersome tax forms and additional taxes sole proprietors and partnerships don't have to deal with, makes incorporating unattractive to most one- and two-person businesses.

If you are running a business by yourself or with your spouse and family, a sole proprietorship is probably the best type of business for you. Keeping your business simple allows you to devote more of your time to making it successful and less time (and frustration) with government regulations and paperwork. However, for individuals in businesses with a high possibility of being sued or in need of raising capital, an S corporation provides some peace of mind because personal assets and credit records are protected. For more detailed information about the three basic types of business and what is required for each, I recommend that you get a copy of the IRS Publication 334, *Tax Guide for Small Business*. This book is essential for anybody starting up a new business. It describes in detail what records must be kept, what deductions are allowed, and how to fill out the various tax forms, and includes many valuable examples. Reading this book should be one of the first things you do before you start up your business. The book is free and you can pick it up at your nearest IRS office or request a copy by mail.

BUSINESS NAME

One of the first things to consider when starting a new business is choosing a name. This can be fun, but you should choose a name with care. I recommend that you pick a name that is simple and easy to pronounce. You don't want people to avoid mentioning your business because the name is difficult or uncomfortable to say. You should also select a name that describes your business, so that potential clients and business associates can easily identify what you do. You may simply use your own name or a part of your name in combination with some descriptive term, such as "William Gordon, Literary Agent" or "Gordon Literary Agency." You may also choose a name unrelated to your own given name, such as "Metropolitan Literary Agency" or "Los Angeles Literary Associates."

As these examples show, you can tag words onto the end of your name such as agency, associates, company, and the like. But you need to be careful with some terms. The word "enterprises" is one of these. Because enterprises can be used with most any type of business, it has been over-used, particularly by one-person businesses and other very small companies. As a result, the word now has become synonymous with "amateur." If you want to avoid being automatically classified as an inexperienced one-person business, you should avoid this term. Other words you should not use are corporation (Corp.), incorporated (Inc.), and limited (Ltd.). These terms all denote a corporation, and your business should be legally incorporated before you use them.

Once you have chosen a name, you must go to your local county clerk's office (this is usually in the county courthouse), register your business name and get a Fictitious Name Statement.

This is discussed in more detail in this chapter in "Licenses and Permits" on page 33.

If you use your own name as a part of your company name, such as John Smith Company, in most places you are not required to get a Fictitious Name Statement. Many localities will waive the registration, even if only your last name is included in the business name. So, Nelson Literary Services would not need to be registered. Check with your local county clerk's office to see what the requirements are in your area.

BUSINESS LOCATION AND ADDRESS

Another important consideration is choosing a business location and address. The two may not be the same. If you work out of your home, your first thought may be to use your home address for business. Although there is nothing wrong with working out of the home, in some types of businesses home-based workers are not taken as seriously or considered as professional or successful as those who can afford an outside office. This is sometimes the case with literary agents. However, many successful agents do work out of their homes. Many people in the literary industry, such as freelance editors, writers, indexers, reviewers, as well as agents, frequently work out of their homes. Most clients realize this and show no prejudice.

Unless you already rent an office outside your home for other purposes, working out of your home is the most convenient and cost effective route you can take. Renting a separate office, especially when you are first starting out and income is at its lowest, is generally an unnecessary luxury and expense.

There are many advantages of working out of a home-based office. Convenience is obviously one of the prime benefits. You can spend as much time at the office as you need with all the conveniences of home. You waste no time commuting to and from work. You have instant access to business records and materials 24 hours a day. Overhead expenses are low. You can take time to attend young children or fill other obligations throughout the day. You are also entitled to some important tax deductions. You can deduct as business expenses a part of your rent and household costs, such as trash removal, gas, and electricity.

If you work at home, you should be aware of zoning laws. Due to zoning laws, technically it is illegal in many residential areas to operate a business out of the home. The zoning laws were established to protect homeowners from businesses that create a lot of noise, attract crowds, or produce offensive odors. Some areas require home-based businesses located in residential zones to obtain some kind of "conditional use," or "special-use" permit. Many home-based workers have challenged zoning laws that prohibit or restrict home businesses and, although they have not always been successful, they have usually been allowed to continue to work at home without legal reprisals so long as there are no complaints from area residents. Barbara Brabec in her book, *Homemade Money,* explains that home-based workers have been able to avoid zoning conflicts by using a post office box as a business address. Since the post office is located in a commercial zone, the business is considered part of that zone. But again, there must not be complaints from the neighbors. The point to this is that, if you don't disturb your neighbors and no one complains about what you are doing, in most cases you can work out of your home regardless of the zoning laws. As a literary agent, you should not be a nuisance to your neighbors and, therefore, do not need to worry about violating your local zoning laws.

You can make your home office appear more businesslike by having a separate business address—one that is not obviously a residential address (e.g., Artistic Cir., Silent Rain Rd., Chestnut Ct., Bluebird Pl., Colony Hills Ln.). This can be done by renting a postal box. Also, if you live in an apartment or move frequently, a postal box provides stability. Some people do not like to use a post office box because they feel it appears less legitimate. The belief is that con artists frequently use them rather than reveal their residence address. This may have been so at one time, but it really isn't true anymore. A great many businesses use post office boxes for their mailing addresses.

Because so many businesses use postal boxes nowadays, there is little prejudice against it. In fact, a post office box can make you look more businesslike because you are not using an obvious residential address.

If you don't want to use your residential address and don't want to use a post office box number, you can use a private postal box. These are very popular because you use the street address where the postal box office is located and a suite number to designate your box number. This way it appears as if your mailing address is an office, rather than a postal box. The cost to rent a private postal box is a little more than a post office box. Private postal boxes can be found in most any moderate-sized city. Look in the phone book under "Mailing Service" for one in your area.

If you are relatively stable in your present location, your residential address looks like it could be a business address, and you do not disturb your neighbors, it is cheaper and easier just to use your residential address.

LICENSES AND PERMITS

Before you can go into business, you must conform to all government laws and regulations. Most licenses and permits are regulated by local governments: city, county, and state. You can expect to pay something for the licenses and permits you need. Fees can run anywhere from $10 to as much as $100 or more. Some home-based businesses ignore these requirements and get away with it, but it is too much of a risk and limits the amount of exposure you can get. If you get too much publicity or too much business, someone is going to find out and you could be hit with a heavy fine or put out of business.

Trade Name Registration

If your business goes by a name other than your own name, you will need to get a fictitious name, also known as DBA, which is an acronym for "doing business as." If you do business under a fictitious name, you are required to register the name in the county in which you do business. This prevents other businesses in the county from doing business under the same name. Before your name can be registered, it must be checked with all the other business names in the county. If the name you have chosen, or a very similar name, is already registered by someone else, you will need to pick another name. If you live in a large metropolitan area, you may find that your first choice is already being used and maybe even your second and third. So you might want to have a few names selected, just in case your first choice is not available. When your business name is cleared and registered, you will receive a Fictitious Name Statement that allows you to do business under that name. In addition to registering your name, you will be required to publish a notice of your business name in a general circulation newspaper. Any advertisement you may plan to run in the paper would satisfy this requirement. But you can fulfill this requirement by placing a small, inexpensive classified ad. The county clerk may even provide you with a list of local newspapers which carry such ads. The cheapest papers to advertise in are usually local publications which are devoted almost entirely to classified advertising.

Registration of your trade name is good for anywhere from five to 10 years, depending on your locality, after which time you will need to renew your registration. If you don't renew your registration, another person can claim your business name and you will be forced to change your company name. Most county offices do not bother to send renewal notices, so you will have to keep track of when your registration expires. Contact your county clerk's office for details.

Business License

Besides the Fictitious Name Statement, most places require businesses to get a local business license. Businesses which use a fictitious name usually must get their Fictitious Name Statement first. All types of businesses are required to get a license. Some occupations, such as accountants, lawyers, chiropractors, doctors, and other professionals are expected to have educational qualifications and are required to pass a test before a license is issued. But for most businesses, including literary representation, no special tests or certifications are required. Business licenses are renewed every year or two.

Sales Tax Permit

Every state which has a sales tax issues a sales tax permit. In most states, service sales are not taxable. But if you sell merchandise along with your service, you must collect sales tax. If you don't sell any products, you don't have to worry about getting a sales tax permit. For more information on the sales tax requirements in your area, contact your state and city revenue offices.

Better Business Bureau

Before doing business with new companies, some people will check with the Better Business Bureau. If the companies are registered and have no complaints filed against them, it is assumed the businesses are legitimate and operating in a proper manner. You can increase your credibility by registering with your local bureau. To register, take your business license down to your local BBB and fill out an application. That's all there is to it. Being registered and having no complaints may be the key that will help you land some important clients.

BANK ACCOUNT

You should open up a separate checking account for your business, rather than use your personal account. The reason for keeping your business and personal finances separate is to have an accurate record of your business finances. Combining the two will only get you confused later on, when you're trying to figure your taxes or your company's financial situation.

If you have chosen a business name other than your own name, you will need to add this name to your bank account so you can deposit checks written out to your business, and so you can get checks with your business name printed on them. The bank needs to know that you and your business are the same, and for verification they will need to see the Fictitious Name Statement you obtained at the county courthouse.

Some banks allow self-employed customers to put their business name on their personal checking account. In this case you can have two personal accounts—one for personal use and one for business. This is the most economical option. Other banks may require you to have an actual business account. This is okay, except that banks usually charge businesses additional or higher processing fees and minimum balances are usually larger, so it will cost you a little more for a business account. Shop around for a bank that will let you use a personal account for your business or one that has the most economical terms for their business accounts.

LETTERHEADS AND ENVELOPES

An important part of your business success depends on the image you present. The way you present yourself influences what people think of you. If you try to look and act like an experienced professional, you will be perceived as one, even if you are a beginner. As a professional, you will be able to interest more people in your services.

One of the best ways to project a positive image is to have professionally-designed letterheads, matching envelopes, and business cards printed using your business name. I stress "professionally-designed" because too many self-employed individuals give little thought to designing a logo or letterhead, and their designs shout "amateur!" Have a graphic artist design your logo and letterhead or ask your printer for suggestions. He may have several suitable styles for you to choose from.

Printed stationery is important because it conveys the image that you are a successful professional. It also lets publishers know that your submissions are from an agent and not an author. It is important to present a proper business appearance and attitude. Include your business name, mailing address, and phone number on all your stationery.

Along with stationery, you will need mailing labels, manila envelopes, mailers, postage scales, and stamps. Since you will probably be doing most of your work for out-of-town clients and publishers, you will be dealing with the mail. Become familiar with the postage prices. The post office distributes a card which lists postage prices for various weights of letters and packages. Knowing the proper postage and stamping your own mailings will keep you from waiting in often tediously long lines at the post office.

TELEPHONE

Most home-based businesses use their residential lines for their business. After all, why pay extra for another phone line when one is already available? I don't recommend this. Phone regulations in each state vary and in some states it is illegal to use your personal line in a business. Depending on your state regulations, you may simply be asked to stop, or you may be charged business phone rates, or be hit with a hefty fine. If you print your phone number on your stationery and business cards (as you should), in advertisements, and answer the phone with a business name, sooner or later you will be discovered. Call your local phone company to find out what the regulations are in your area.

Using your residential phone in your business does not qualify it for a tax deduction. The first phone line in the home cannot be used as a tax deduction. A second line can be fully deductible if it is used primarily for your business. In states where business can be conducted over a residential line, you can have two personal lines and designate one as your business line. Of course, all long-distance business calls are deductible regardless of which phone is used.

The phone you use in business should be answered with the business name and not with a simple "Hello." This is all part of conducting yourself in a businesslike manner and conveying a professional image. If one of your children answers the phone, the caller may think he has the wrong number or question if you are running a serious business. This may cause a potential client to go elsewhere. You cannot simply tell your family not to answer the phone during certain hours. Calls are not restricted to just business hours or on weekdays. Although most business calls come during normal working hours, you may receive calls at any hour and on weekends and holidays.

I recommend that you get a separate business line regardless of the state regulations. One major advantage of having a business line is that your phone number will be listed in the business section of the phone book. People looking for literary agents often look in the phone book first. Plus, local and out-of-state callers can get in touch with you by asking for directory assistance. Not having a business listing is a serious mistake because it will stifle business opportunities and prevent many potential clients from getting in contact with you. Although the monthly fee for a business phone is a little higher, there is no additional charge for the basic yellow page listing. The small extra cost of having a business line is well worth it.

You have three options available to you: (1) add a business line (the best option), (2) use a second personal line for business (if state laws permit), or (3) remove your personal line and install a single business line. The third option avoids the cost of having a second line and gets your company listed in the *Yellow Pages*. However, as a signle line, you cannot deduct the basic phone cost on your taxes and you must constantly regulate who answers the phone.

Another consideration you need to make is using an answering machine or answering service. Having an answering machine is important to a one-person business since you cannot be home all the time to answer your phone. With an answering machine, clients can leave messages with assurance that their calls will be returned. This prevents them from recalling needlessly or from going elsewhere with their business.

RECORD-KEEPING AND TAXES

Bookkeeping

Bookkeeping is an often dreaded but necessary aspect of business. You must keep accurate records not only for tax purposes, but to help you operate your business. Many of your business decisions will be based on your financial records. Carefully reviewing these records may be the only way you will really know if you're making a profit or not. Many business failures have been attributed to poor record-keeping. This is particularly important with home-based businesses, where personal and business finances can become mixed and confused.

Keeping an accurate financial record is not really difficult. You do not need an accountant to keep your books. All you need to do is keep a daily record of all your business income and expenses. Buy a ledger book at an office supply store to record expenses and income. Every time you have a business expense or receive payment, write it down. Write it down that day; do not wait or you may forget to enter it. Keeping your records accurate should be a daily practice that should take you only a few minutes.

All business transactions should be made through your business checking account. When you receive a payment, deposit it in your account. Pay all your business expenses with a business check. This way your income and expenses are easily recorded and well-documented. You may not, however, be able to pay all of your expenses by check. Some payments will have to be in cash, such as a parking fee. Make sure that these expenses are recorded in your expense ledger and receipts are kept for everything, including credit card purchases.

Keep a file and put all of your receipts in it. You must have proof for each expense you claim as a deduction. If you are audited, you will be required to produce these receipts. You will need to keep these records for at least three years because audits can go back that far.

Some agents bill their clients for certain expenses involved in marketing their works, such as postage and phone calls. Include this provision in the contract you sign with the author, and use an invoice. If you bill your clients for these expenses, you need to keep a careful record of the invoices you send out and keep track of payments received. Expenses that are reimbursed by your clients cannot be used as deductions on your income tax unless you include the payments as part of your income. You can buy standard invoice forms at an office supply store or have personalized invoices printed with your business name.

Payments from publishers are outlined in the publishing agreements and are usually paid twice a year. A contract may specify that royalties earned for all books sold between January through June be paid by August of that same year. A few months' leeway is given so that the publisher has time to evaluate sales and calculate payments for each six-month period.

For income tax purposes, you have to choose an accounting method. The two primary accounting methods are cash and accrual. One of these methods is chosen when you file your first tax return for your business. After that, you must use the same method every year. If you want to change your accounting method, you must first get permission from the IRS.

The cash method of accounting is used by most individuals and many small, service-oriented businesses. If you sell a product, rather than or in addition to a service, you are required to use the accrual method.

In the cash method of accounting, income is recorded when cash is received and expenses are recorded when paid. Cash is defined as currency, checks, and money orders. All credit purchases and sales are not recorded until payment is received. This is an easy method of accounting, but not totally representative of your financial situation because you may have debts or unpaid credit accounts that are not taken into consideration.

In the accrual method of accounting, income and expenses are recorded when they are incurred, regardless of when they are paid. When you bill a client for services, you will record it in your income ledger as income. When you make a credit purchase, you will record that as an expense when the purchase is made and not when it is paid.

As a service business, if most of your income is received on a cash basis, it might be better for you to use the cash method of accounting. If you routinely extend credit to clients, you might consider using the accrual method.

Taxes

You can deduct, on your income tax return, any expenses related to operating your business—postage, stationery, typing or other services you use, travel expenses, gasoline usage, phone, insurance, advertising, bad debts, professional services, taxes and licenses, etc. Any business expense is legitimate. If you have an office in your home, exclusively set aside for your business, you can deduct the rent or part of the mortgage payment for that portion of your home. You also can deduct a portion of your expenses for household utilities (water, electricity, gas). To do this, though, the room must be used exclusively for your business and nothing else.

Your total business income is figured by subtracting all your business expenses from your business income. One advantage of being self-employed is that a net loss in your business can offset other income. For example, if at year end you had a net loss of $2,000 from your home business, but earned $20,000 as an employee in another business, your total income would be $18,000. To prevent people from claiming business losses every year as a result of an activity that is really a hobby rather than a legitimate business, the IRS has put some limitations on the self-employed. To use a net loss to offset other income, a business must keep accurate records, conduct itself in a businesslike manner, and make a profit in at least three out of five consecutive years.

In spite of some business owner's best efforts, a profit may not be realized in the time specified. For this reason, the IRS has allowed some exceptions to the three-years-of-profit test. The determining factors will be if your activity is carried on in a businesslike manner, you spend adequate time to make it successful, income is used for your livelihood, you have adequate experience in this activity, and you can expect to make a profit in the future.

For further information on business deductions and how to figure your net income or loss, I highly recommend that you read the IRS publication, *Tax Guide for Small Business* (Publication 334) and *Business Use of Your Home* (Publication 587). You need to do this before you start spending any money in your business so you will be aware of what you can and what you can't deduct, and what will be expected of you when you figure your income tax return.

Because you are self-employed, you will not receive W-2 forms from any of the clients or publishers with whom you work. W-2 forms are given to employees only. However, publishers may send you a 1099 form, which reports royalty payments. Like W-2 forms, these payments are reported to the IRS. You will not have deductions taken out of the money you receive, so you need to keep track of how much you earn and how much tax you need to pay. If you earn a substantial amount, your tax obligation could be significant. To ease the burden of paying a large amount of taxes at the end of the year, the IRS requires payment of estimated taxes. These are paid quarterly throughout the tax year. The IRS provides form 1040ES for this purpose.

OPERATING A HOME-BASED BUSINESS

Being self-employed requires dedication and self-discipline. When working out of the home, you can easily be distracted by non-business activities. To avoid distractions and make your time productive, you should first have an area in your home set aside exclusively as your office. Preferably, this should be in an area of the house where you are away from the television and other possible distractions. Because the home is usually a place of relaxation, especially after working all day for someone else, you may have a hard time mustering the enthusiasm to work and thus have a tendency to waste time. As you establish a habit of working in your home office, it will be easier to get into the mood of working. The second thing you should do is set up a work schedule and stick to it. Set aside specific times each day as your work hours. Let your family and friends know that you can't be disturbed during this time. Following these two suggestions will help you become more productive and avoid wasting time, but it is not a guarantee of success. Your business will only be as successful as you make it. The amount of time and effort you spend and your enthusiasm will determine the degree of success you achieve.

Besides spending time, you will need to spend some money. It is a general rule that making money requires spending money. Home-based businesses are no different. Some home-based businesses require a substantial outlay of capital, while others require almost none. Fortunately, a literary agency can be set up with a minimal amount of investment. Since you work out of your home, your overhead expenses are minor. Your initial expenses will be the purchase of stationery, ledgers for record-keeping, and initial advertising. Your biggest expense will be in marketing your services. This includes the cost of producing flyers, sales letters, and brochures, as well as postage, telephone expenses, and the like. Advertising and marketing your services are discussed more fully in the next chapter.

On average, it takes about two years for a new business to develop efficient operating procedures and build up a customer base. Unless you already have extensive experience working in a literary agency or publishing company, it will probably take you at least this long. Because of start-up costs and inexperience, most small businesses do not make a profit until their second or third year of operation. As a literary agent, your start-up costs will be minimal. Since your home will probably serve as your base of operations, you will not have the overhead expenses other businesses have. But you will have to spend time and money building up a clientele. As you gain experience finding new customers and building up your customer base, your income will increase. It will be slow at first, but if you are dedicated and not easily discouraged, your chances of finding success will be good. One of the drawbacks for people starting new businesses is staying enthused and optimistic during the first slow months. You may seem to be putting more time and money into the business than it is worth. But this happens to almost all new businesses. So don't get discouraged. It may take you a few years to build up your business to the point where you are making a reasonable income. Few businesses are overnight successes, especially home-based businesses, so give it time.

Books I highly recommend for helping you set up and run a successful home-based business are *Homemade Money* and *Help for Your Growing Homebased Business,* both by Barbara Brabec, and *Small-Time Operator* by Bernard Kamoroff. Another excellent resource is Barbara Brabec's *Self-Employment Survival Letter,* a newsletter written specifically for people who are self-employed. It discusses the problems and challenges self-employed and home-based workers face, and provides solutions and networking opportunities. For further information, write to Barbara Brabec's Self-Employment Survival Letter, P.O. Box 2137, Naperville, IL 60567.

Chapter 4

SERVICES AND FEES

In this chapter you will learn about one of the most important parts of being a literary agent—the financial rewards. You will also learn some of the important services agents can provide clients to enhance their chances of getting published.

COMMISSIONS AND FEES

Literary agents are paid 10-25 percent commission on sales they make, 10-15 percent being the most common for sales within the country, and 20-25 percent for sales outside the country. The standard commission once was 10 percent, but 15 percent is becoming more prevalent among literary agents. Ten percent is still standard for script agents on domestic sales and 15 percent for foreign sales.

The commission is paid on all royalties earned by the author, including the advance. The publisher sends the royalty check to the agent, who deducts his commission and forwards the rest to the author. If, for instance, an agent charges a 15 percent commission and the author receives a total of $10,000, the agent's earnings would be $1,500. If the book happens to be a very good seller and earns $100,000, the agent gets $15,000—not a bad profit on a single book. You can imagine the potential with a million-copy bestseller!

Established literary agents, like publishers, are flooded with unsolicited manuscripts. For this reason, they spend most of their time reading rather than marketing books. Although they may be representing 20 or 30 different clients at a time, not all of the manuscripts they work with get published. Because of this, many agents supplement their commission income by charging the authors fees for various services.

Almost all agents charge a *marketing fee*, as it is frequently called. This fee is paid to reimburse the agent for expenses in marketing the author's work. It could be paid in a lump sum or billed as expenses occur. It will include postage, phone and fax, photocopying, express mail expenses, and the like. A set amount, such as $20 or $40, may be charged for each book the agent represents, or the agent may bill the author for the actual expenses. Unless there are some unusual expenses that are authorized by the author, marketing expenses should not exceed more than about $50. Some agents deduct fees out of royalties, and others may even refund the fees if the manuscript is sold.

Only a fraction of the hundreds of manuscripts sent to publishers are accepted for publication. The vast majority of those that are accepted are from seasoned writers who have had other works published. Most new writers have not yet developed their writing skills well enough to get published. The chances of an agent finding a salable manuscript among unpublished authors are slim in comparison to published authors, and offers from publishers for works by first-time authors are usually less. For these reasons, many well-established and successful literary agents and agencies will not even consider representing unpublished authors.

Smaller and newer agencies, however, have to build up their clientele and so they are much more willing to work with unpublished authors. There are hundreds of thousands of unpublished authors seeking publication of their works. Most of their manuscripts are unpublishable. Agents are swamped with submissions from these people. It is impossible to evaluate all of them. Since agents make their money on commissions from sales, it is a waste of their time to evaluate every submission they receive. Material from current clients and other published authors receives priority.

To weed out curiosity seekers or writers who don't have much faith in their own works, most agents who are willing to work with unpublished authors charge a "reading fee". The reading fee is paid to the agent just to have him read the manuscript. There is no promise that the agent will represent the author, nor is the agent obligated or expected to evaluate the manuscript or make any suggestions for improvement. The fee is paid simply to compensate the agent for his time spent in reading. This one-time fee for unpublished authors can vary anywhere from $40 to $400 or more. Some agents require reading fees from all potential clients unless the author has had several books successfully published. If the agent feels the manuscript can be sold, he will offer to represent the author and attempt to sell it to a publisher. Whether the agent accepts the manuscript or not, he is still paid the reading fee. Sometimes the agent will refund the fee if he agrees to represent the author or if the manuscript sells. The agent may do the reading himself or hire a "reader" to do it. The reader weeds out all unsalable manuscripts and passes on to the agent those that show some promise. The agent then examines these and chooses the ones he believes he could successfully market.

Sometimes the reading fee is referred to as an "evaluation fee". In this case, the agent will write a report evaluating the manuscript's literary strengths, weaknesses, and marketing potential. The evaluation can vary from one paragraph to several detailed pages. The more work involved, the higher the fee. Evaluation fees range as high as $300-$400 or more. Usually a manuscript evaluation or critique is offered as a separate service, and the author may be charged a reading fee with the option of also receiving a critique if desired. Most agents offer consultation services, which are available to anybody. This service is to advise authors who are not clients on book contracts for manuscripts sold without the help of an agent. These fees range from $20-$200 per hour. Many publishers who have accepted works from unagented authors request that they find agents to work with before negotiating the publishing agreement. Publishers prefer to work with agents because authors are generally unfamiliar with contracts and terms of negotiation. Agents know which terms of the contract can be negotiated and which are the most important. Unlike a busy editor with deadlines to meet, an agent can spend more time helping the author understand contract negotiations and answering the many questions new authors frequently ask.

LITERARY SERVICES

The primary function of a literary agent is to represent the author and sell his or her work at the best terms possible. Agents who represent only well-known writers have a relatively easy time selling their clients' works. Agents who routinely represent unpublished authors work harder to make each sale. Many are compensated for their time in part by charging new writers reading and evaluation fees. Most authors can greatly benefit from a variety of services not always offered by the big literary agencies. These services will help an author improve his writing skill, polish his manuscript, and make it more salable, thus increasing his chances of getting published.

New writers often need a little editorial assistance to improve their books. Naturally, this extra service will require some additional payment. The agent must pay for these services or be compensated for his time if he performs them himself. Some high-brow agents who represent only established authors look down on agents who offer these services. But agents who offer these services are the ones willing to take a risk and represent new writers, and the ones who help new writers improve their skills so that they can become successful authors.

This section discusses some of the helpful services agents can offer their clients. If the agent is qualified, he may perform these services himself. If not, there are many freelancers available willing to work with agents and authors.

Making Good Manuscripts Great

Book publisher Alfred A. Knopf said, "We have now reached a point where it becomes more and more difficult to get a reasonable hearing for a book that is simply good—not a world-shattering masterpiece, not the choice of a major book club, not to be made into a super-colossal movie, but just a good book which several thousand [people] would probably read with pleasure and profit from if they ever laid hold of it."

Knopf reveals an interesting aspect of book publishing. Not all *good* books get published. What gets accepted and what gets rejected is often based on the gut feeling of the editor. In considering two manuscripts for publication when only one can be accepted, the editor must choose the one which has the greatest chance for success. If the manuscripts have equal potential, the deciding factor will likely rest with the quality of the work. This might include the author's ability to express himself clearly and accurately, the scholarship of the research, and the amount of editing necessary to prepare it for publication.

Many services are available to help writers improve their work and increase their chances of getting published. With competition as stiff as it is, agents should encourage authors to take advantage of any opportunity they can to improve their works. Doing so could easily make the difference between receiving a rejection notice or a royalty check.

Critiquing Service

Some agents offer a critiquing service for their clients. This involves not only reading the manuscript, but writing a detailed evaluation or critique for the author. The terms "critique" and "evaluation" are sometimes used interchangeably, although a critique usually involves a more extensive evaluation and detailed report recommending ways to improve the work.

When material is rejected by editors at publishing houses, the writer almost never receives an evaluation of the manuscript or an explanation for the rejection other than being told that it "does not meet our current needs." That's all. You will have no idea why it was rejected. Only rarely will the editor have liked the material enough to take the time to write you a personal rejection letter and perhaps hint at some areas which need improvement.

In most cases, you will have no idea why an editor rejects the manuscript. You will keep resubmitting the same manuscript to other publishers who may all reject it for the same reasons. It may not be a bad manuscript. In fact, it may be very good, but have some drawbacks that a little rewriting would correct.

A literary critic can point out flaws or problems in a manuscript. Some literary critics prefer to call themselves manuscript analysts, writing consultants, or book doctors. Whatever name they go by, a literary critic can identify problems, make suggestions for improvement, and offer helpful advice that could make a significant improvement in the manuscript. Although a critic will not point out every misspelled word, incorrect use of punctuation, poor use of grammar, or other mechanical problems, he will note that such problems exist. The major function of the critic is to evaluate the text in terms of the author's writing style and execution. This evaluation should consist of several pages, although comments could be made directly in the text as well.

A critic looks for many things when evaluating a manuscript. Is the author's writing clear? Would readers understand the descriptions and explanations? (This is particularly important with a how-to or self-help type of book.) Is the vocabulary consistent and appropriate for the readership? (A research scientist writing a book for general audiences would lose readers if he used too much scientific terminology.) Is the material interesting? Does it make the reader want to read more? If it is nonfiction, are the facts and findings presented in an interesting way? Is there supplementary material? (This includes maps, charts, graphs, illustrations, appendix, references, index, footnotes, bibliography, etc.) Are they necessary? Are they adequate or incomplete? Are they effectively and properly presented? Do they make a statement or just fill space? For a novel, is the plot and/or subplot(s) clearly defined? Are characters adequately developed? Is suspense or interest maintained throughout the story? Does everything make sense? Is the story believable? Are the facts correct or realistic?

A literary critic can increase a manuscript's chances of publication by pointing out problems in all these areas. However, some authors feel that a critic's honest, professional feedback is disheartening and overly negative. Most writers take pride in their work and tend to seek praise, not criticism. If the evaluation is not complimentary, it is often ignored and the writer feels discouraged or even cheated because he did not receive what he wanted. If you use a critique service, you must tell your client to have an open mind and accept criticism. If the author has questions about the critique, be willing to discuss them with him. If you and the author doubt some of the critic's recommendations or comments, that is okay. Whether or not the author follows the critic's advice is up to him, and the author must make the final decision himself.

Fees for critiquing services can be based on page or word count. The amount charged varies according to the detail of the critique. Criticism fees can range up to $400 or more. If the you have the experience and training to qualify as a literary critic, you can perform this service yourself. If not, many freelance critiquing services are available.

Copyediting and Proofreading Services

Having a knowledgeable editor read and correct a work is the most valuable service an author can receive. While a literary critic makes suggestions on revisions concerning content and style, an editor actually makes detailed corrections in the text.

Proofreaders look for and correct spelling, punctuation, grammatical, typographical, and other mechanical errors. A copyeditor's job includes everything a proofreader does, but goes one step further. In addition to making mechanical corrections, the copyeditor corrects literary errors. This includes correcting inconsistencies in style, awkward sentence structure, and clarifying sentences, words, or ideas not clearly expressed by the writer. The copyeditor works on sentence structure, phrases, and word choice to make the text flow smoother.

Although agents do not routinely edit their client's manuscripts, they may offer copyediting and proofreading as a separate service. The cost for a freelance editor to copyedit a manuscript ranges from about $6-$30 per hour or $1-$5 per page, based on the subject of the work and degree of editing performed. Proofreading costs somewhat less than a detailed editing job. If the agent performs this work himself or hires outside editorial help, this expense is charged to the author.

Editorial help, copyediting and proofreading, not only improve the manuscript, but greatly improve the chances of having the work accepted for publication. One of the primary reasons manuscripts are rejected is that they do not meet the standards of publication. Publishers receive so many manuscripts that they can be very choosy. Some are extremely picky and do not even consider material that is not close to being perfect. Years ago, editors were willing to work with authors with good ideas and potential, but in need of a little editorial help. Nowadays, however, editors can't afford to spend time tutoring authors or doctoring manuscripts.

Every writer, no matter what his skill level is, can benefit by having his work reviewed by an experienced copyeditor. When I say experienced copyeditor, I don't mean friends or relatives who are not sufficiently qualified. They may catch obvious errors, but there is much more to proofreading and copyediting than spotting simple typographical errors. Also, beware of depending too much on computer software programs designed to check for spelling and grammatical errors. Such programs should not be a substitute for having material proofread. Computer programs will catch simple errors, but pass over words spelled correctly but used incorrectly. It takes a human to catch these types of errors.

Copyediting provides a second educated opinion or viewpoint. Many statements that make sense to the writer may not be clear to someone who is unfamiliar with the subject. A copyeditor can point out these problems. Writers become so familiar with their own material that they tend to see only what they want to see. They can read their material over and over, looking for errors, and then hand it to someone else who may quickly point out obvious typos. This sort of thing happens to all writers.

If you are working with a successful author who has no trouble getting published without using editorial services, then he probably doesn't need them. But most unpublished authors can benefit greatly by having their work checked by a competent copyeditor or proofreader.

Typing Services

Some agents offer their clients typing or manuscript preparation services. Many new writers do not know how to prepare a book proposal or manuscript properly. As a literary agent, you should know how to prepare this material in a professional manner (see Chapter 8) and be willing to help your clients.

Submissions must be set up in proper format and neatly typed. Some people still use old, outdated typewriters that produce uneven lines and blurry type. Others use hard-to-read dot-matrix computer printers. Submissions produced from this type of equipment will either be rejected or given little serious consideration. Editors have too many submissions to evaluate to waste time on those that are hard to read or are not presented in a professional manner.

Agents with letter-quality printers or laser printers can retype their clients' materials or recommend they have it done by a typing service. Some typing services will also check spelling and grammar or edit the material as well. Fees range from about $1-$3 per page.

Publicity Services

Despite the news reports of authors receiving huge advances, most publishers operate on a narrow profit margin. They don't have enough money to advertise and publicize all of their books as they should. In fact, about 90 percent of their publicity budget goes into about 10 percent of their books. Only those books which are considered the most promising and for which the publisher has paid large advances receive any significant promotion. The rest of their books receive little more notice than being mentioned in the publisher's catalog. No book receives the promotion it really deserves. And most books go out of print after the first printing.

To stimulate sales, some agents also offer publicity services. If the publisher doesn't publicize the book, it is up to the author or the agent to do so. The agent can do this by sending news releases to book reviewers, reporters, newspaper and magazine columnists; by booking authors on radio and television talk shows; by arranging autograph-signings at bookstores; and by other publicity-generating activities.

It is in the best interest of author, agent, and publisher to get as much publicity as possible. Authors and agents who have publicized their own books have, at times, saved them from going out of print and, in some cases, propelled them to bestseller status.

An agent can perform this service himself or hire a publicity agent. Resources helpful for understanding how to generate your own publicity include: *Writing Effective News Releases* by Catherine V. McIntyre, *Book Publicity for Authors and Publishers* by Larry J. Rochester, *The Publicity Manual* by Kate Kelly, *Publicity for Books and Authors* by Peggy Glenn, *How to Get Publicity* by William Parkhurst, *The Unabashed Self-Promoter's Guide* by Jeffrey Lant, and *On the Air* by Al Parinello.

Besides promoting your client's published books, you may also consider generating publicity before the manuscript is sold. The author may speak or lecture on his subject to interested groups, get endorsements for his book from recognized professionals, and receive media attention. Doing all this and more is discussed in the books mentioned above. If other people have shown an interest in the author or the subject, editors will also take an interest.

Where to Find Help

In this chapter I have discussed many different types of services that will improve or enhance your client's work. You can find the individuals and companies who offer many of these services in the directory, *Literary Market Place*. This reference book lists publishers, literary agents, copyeditors, ghost writers, publicity agents, manuscript analysts, and many other companies and services involved in the book industry. This directory is expensive, so you're not likely to find it in a bookstore. Most good-sized libraries will have a copy in their reference section. Another, more economically priced, directory which lists writing services is the *Book Publishing Resource Guide*.

The Editorial Freelancers Association (36 E. St., Rm 9R, New York, NY 10036) and the Freelance Editorial Association (P.O. Box 835, Cambridge, MA 02238) can provide you with a list of people offering editorial services.

Another source for these services is writers' magazines. Look in the back of the magazines in the classified ad section. Often the ad listings are categorized so that if you want to find research services, look under "Research," or find copyediting services under "Editing/Revising", and so forth. Magazines also contain ads from literary agents and typing services, as well as writers' workshops and correspondence schools and seminars. These magazines provide an abundance of information that can be beneficial to you and your clients.

Chapter 5

HOW TO FIND CLIENTS

As an agent, you will have many opportunities to discover talented new writers and to help them develop and achieve publishing success. This will bring you great satisfaction, as well as monetary rewards.

In previous chapters, you have learned that it is difficult for most new authors to sell their manuscripts directly to publishers. The larger publishing houses won't even consider material which is not handled by an agent. Publishers often give little attention to unsolicited submissions or to material from unpublished authors. Authors are sent impersonal rejection letters, and sometimes manuscripts are even returned unread. It seems that the only way a new author can overcome this barrier is to have an agent. Consequently, many writers consider an agent to be the solution to getting published.

Most new authors dream of having a national bestseller, and have faith that their book will be a huge success. They believe their works are rejected by publishers only because they are new authors without an agent. They reason that, with an agent, their writings will be given an unbiased evaluation, and publishers will jump at the chance to buy them. Many agents, like publishers, do not like to work with unpublished authors because most of their material is unmarketable. Finding an agent willing to work with a new writer is difficult. For this reason, many authors are looking for agents willing to represent them. This is good for you because it means that you do not have to spend much time or money finding potential clients. They are looking for you! On the other hand, you must realize that you will be approached by many writers who have unsalable material. You must pick and choose whom to work with, or you will spend too much time marketing manuscripts that will never sell.

Unless you have more clients than you can handle, you should never refuse to represent an author simply because he is unpublished. Many skillful unpublished authors are seeking to sell their first book. Some of these people have developed their skills in the course of their professions (e.g., journalism, teaching, copywriting, etc.). Some novice authors may not be able to write a novel like Ernest Hemingway, but they may have the writing skill and knowledge to produce a marketable nonfiction book. Some potentially great writers may be in the developing stages of their careers and may just need a little help from an agent who can provide editorial assistance. There are a few fortunate authors whose first books become bestsellers. Most successful authors, however, build their careers slowly and achieve writing acclaim only after having written several books. Many never write national bestsellers, yet have successful writing careers.

Not all writers who are looking for agents are unpublished. Many writers who have sold their own works or who have become dissatisfied with their present agent are seeking a new agent. Some potential clients may be successful journalists or freelance magazine writers who have yet to sell a book.

Your first priority as a new literary agent is to find clients. If you've worked in the book publishing industry (i.e., editor, sales rep, etc.), you may know authors who are in need of, or are looking for, an agent. Because of your experience in publishing, you have the credentials to convince successful authors to work with you. These are the first people you should approach. If you don't have prior industry experience, you must start from the bottom and work your way up. It is not likely that you will land a famous author or some other celebrity. They already have agents or connections with the large, well-established agencies. You must concentrate on finding people who are relatively new to book publishing, people who have just written their first book or who have had one or more books published but with only modest success.

Authors are seeking you. All you need to do is to let them know where you are. At first, you may need to advertise your existence. In time, you should be listed in important directories, have organizational affiliations, and clients who will let others know about you.

WORD-OF-MOUTH

Clients who are satisfied with the work you do for them will remain with you for many years. In fact, once you have become established, a large majority of the material you market will be from clients you have worked with previously. It costs more, in both time and money, to find a new client than it does to work with an old one. Once you begin working with a successful author, selling additional works by him or her will be easier and usually command higher advances and/or royalties. That is why most agents prefer to work with authors who have already been published. Many agents will not even consider a new client unless he or she has some writing credits. For the reasons I've mentioned here, it is important that you develop a good relationship with your clients and work hard on their behalf so they will stay with you.

Many successful agents rely almost totally on referrals from satisfied clients and professional associates for the majority of their new clients. If a client is happy with the work you do for him, he will be eager to recommend you to other writers.

It is to your advantage to do a professional job in representing each of your authors. An agent who must continually find new clients to produce income (because of incompetence, poor attitude, incompatibility, or laziness) will not be successful. You don't need to depend entirely on your clients to give you word-of-mouth advertising. Use your own mouth to let people know who you are and what you do. The word will spread and people will contact you. Introduce yourself to local English professors, librarians, book dealers, newspaper reporters, and editors. Although these people may not be looking for an agent themselves, they come into contact with writers and potential writers all the time. If you make a good impression, they will pass your name on to interested individuals. Make sure to give out your business cards liberally—that's why you have them.

You might consider contacting local writers' support groups. These groups meet regularly to talk about different aspects of the writing profession, give encouragement, and critique each other's work. These groups consist of both published and unpublished writers. Introduce yourself to them. You might even offer to give them a free short seminar on some aspect of getting published or have a question-and-answer session. You can find local groups by asking your librarian or local high school or college English teachers if they know of writers' groups in your area.

DIRECTORY LISTINGS

The most important directory you can be listed in is the phone book. If you have a business phone, you will automatically be listed in the *Yellow Pages* under the heading "Literary Agents." Most people go to the phone book when they need to find a certain type of business. If you don't live in a very large metropolitan area, particularly New York, Los Angeles, Chicago (the major publishing centers of the U.S.), Toronto (Canada), London (U.K.), or Sydney (Australia) only a few literary agents will be listed. This means that if you are listed, most local authors looking for an agent in the phone book will contact you. Although authors do not need to work with local agents, many people feel more comfortable working with someone they can talk to in person. Personal contact also helps to build up author-agent relations.

You may enhance your telephone listing by getting it printed in bold letters, giving it more space and adding a few extra lines, or even buying a display ad. If there are only a couple of agents listed in your local phone book, it may not be worth the expense to pay for anything more than your name printed in bold type.

There are several other directories that contain extensive listings of literary agents. When searching for agents, writers are usually directed to these sources by librarians and publishing professionals. It is to your advantage to get listed in as many of these as you can.

The most complete and widely used directories are:

Literary Agents of North America
Author Aid/Research Associates International
340 E. 52nd St.
New York, NY 10022

Guide to Literary Agents and Art/Photo Reps
Writer's Digest Books
1507 Dana Avenue
Cincinnati, OH 45207

Literary Market Place
R.R. Bowker
121 Chanlon Road
New Providence, NJ 07974

Directory of Book Publishing
Oryx Press
4041 N. Central
Phoenix, AZ 85012

International Writers' & Artists' Yearbook
A&C Black Ltd.
35 Bedford Row, London, WC1 4JH
England

A couple of other books which, among other things, contain listings of agents are *Insider's Guide to Book Editors, Publishers, and Literary Agents*, by Jeff Herman and *Literary Agents: A Writer's Guide*, by Adam Begley. Most of the books mentioned here can be located in the reference section of your local library. To get your agency included, write to the publishers for listing information. Be aware that many of these directories, before listing new agencies, require them to provide evidence of recent sales. In this case, until you are successful enough to qualify to be listed in these directories, you will have to depend on other forms of advertising to get clients.

ADVERTISING

One of the prime advantages literary agencies have over most other businesses is that publicity and advertising expenses are comparatively small. In fact, most of your advertising budget should be spent in a *Yellow Pages* listing, as it will be one of your most valuable publicity tools. The only other type of advertising you might consider is placing a classified or small display ad in a trade magazine, particularly when you are first starting out.

Advertising expenses should be small because authors are always seeking agents, and they will seek you out. If you are listed in one or more agent directories, they will contact you. Listings are free. Besides the phone book, a listing in these directories will be your best form of advertising.

The problem new agents face with directories is that to be listed, you must give references. If you are just starting out you won't have any. While your business is still young, you will need to do some advertising to build up a clientele and develop the needed references.

Classified Advertising

Classified ads are the least expensive type of paid advertising. You are usually charged so much per word. This figure can vary from a few cents to several dollars per word, depending on the circulation of the publication. The larger the circulation, the more people the ad reaches and the more the publication charges for advertising.

You can advertise in newspapers or magazines. If you are interested in the local market, you can use the newspaper or a local magazine. However, you can get a better response by selecting appropriate national magazines—magazines whose readership is composed of the type of people who would most likely use your services. It would be unproductive to advertise in *Popular Mechanics* or *Brewery Digest.* Instead, look for consumer and trade magazines aimed at writers. A list of appropriate magazines can be found in the directory *Writer's Market.* This book is discussed in more detail in Chapter 7.

Once you have a list of magazines, write to the advertising department and ask for classified advertising rates and deadline dates. You will receive material providing you with the prices and dates for several months or a full year. You will also note that most of the larger magazines require that your ad be sent in about two months before publication.

Some of these magazines even have subheadings in the classified section for editors, indexers, critiquing services, etc. Look at the ads in writers' magazines for examples of classified ads. Model your ad after those which most impress you. Keep your ad brief and to the point.

Typically, the cost for classified advertising runs about $4-$8 per word. This includes your address, phone number, zip code—everything. Once you start writing the ad, you will discover it is quite easy to say too much and end up with an ad that costs $300 or more. With a little rewriting and editing, you can trim your ad down to the bare bones. To keep expenses down, say just enough to get your message across, but no more than necessary. In the ad below, there are 42 words. Assuming $4 a word, it would cost $168 to run this ad in one issue of a publication.

Lawrence Literary Agency now accepting new clients. Looking for novels, children's books, plays, how-to, self-help, and all types of nonfiction. Represents many first-time authors. For more information, send query and SASE to Matthew Lawrence Literary Agency, 639 Upton Avenue, Stockton, CA 95825.

The following ad says basically the same thing as the one above, but with only 22 words for a cost of only $88.

Literary representation; new writers welcome; mainstream fiction and nonfiction; no poetry; query first; SASE. Lawrence Literary Agency, 639 Upton, Stockton, CA 95825.

Following are some examples of the type of ads agents run. Look in the writers' magazines for additional examples.

Literary agent seeking new clients, fiction and nonfiction, query, SASE.

Manuscripts wanted. Fiction/nonfiction. No reading fee. Query or manuscript. SASE.

National literary agency looking for new authors. Novels, screenplays, biographies. Evaluation and editing services available. SASE free information.

Sci-Fi and mystery novels—will help you sell yours. Professional representation. Send query and complete manuscript including SASE.

Display Advertising

Display ads can range from one inch in height by one column in width to a full page. Unlike classified ads, which are grouped together at the end of the publication, display ads are normally scattered throughout. Usually, the advertiser will prepare his own ad to fit the space purchased. Since visual impact is important, most display ads contain a mixture of text and graphics designed to attract the reader's attention.

Prices of display ads are based on two factors—size and circulation. The cost is lowest for small ads and gets progressively more expensive with size. The price difference between a one-inch and a full-page ad could be several thousand dollars. The other factor which affects price is the circulation size of the publication. The larger the circulation, the more expensive the ad. It may cost tens of thousands of dollars to place a single full-page ad in a popular magazine. On the other hand, the same ad run in a relatively small-circulation periodical may cost only a couple of hundred dollars.

For a literary agency, large display ads are too expensive and unnecessary. Smaller, cheaper ads will bring you just about as good a response as a larger one. People are either interested or they aren't. It is not like advertising soap or some other product where space is important. Commercial ads must first attract the reader's eye, then sell the product. A literary agent is looking for people who need and want his services. These people will easily spot your ad because of their interest.

In most cases, I would not recommend using a display ad unless it is small and inexpensive. The only possible exception would be in a small circulation publication that has a very specific readership—one composed of writers, particularly new writers who do not already have agents.

Another option you might consider is a classified/display ad. This is a hybrid of the two, but not all publications offer this option. Frequently, it is restricted to one area of the publication which is divided into categories like ordinary classified ads, but you buy space and have your own ad printed. Ads vary in size from one column inch to three or four inches or more. Ads can be simple text, like a classified ad, or contain eye-catching type and graphics. Cost is much more reasonable than an ordinary display ad. Some writers' magazines offer classified/display ad space with headings such as "Literary Agents" and "Literary Services." Concerned readers can focus on ads of interest. Some of the writers' publications advise readers of their classified or display/classified sections to request a list of manuscripts the agent has sold within the last two years, their authors, where placed, and the publication dates. This is done to help readers avoid dishonest or inept agents. You will find that many conscientious writers request this information before working with an agent. As you build up your business, you will want to keep track of this information, so that it is readily available when requested.

PROFESSIONAL ORGANIZATIONS

Literary agents learn their trade by experience. They are not required to have any special training or accreditation. Membership in trade organizations, however, requires them to adhere to a code of ethics and standards, giving them some degree of recognition as professionals.

The major organization for agents is the Association of Authors' Representatives (AAR). This organization strives to uphold professional standards and ethics. All new members are expected to meet certain professional qualifications. Applicants are required to ask two present members of the AAR to nominate them for membership by writing letters of recommendation. Candidates are expected to have a minimum of two years' prior experience and (for literary agents) be able to list 10 or more books sold in the last 18 months or (for script agents) list at least five productions in the last 24 months. An initiation fee and annual dues must accompany the application form. The application and letters of recommendation are reviewed by the Board of Directors, who may ask for additional information before a final decision is made. Their address is: AAR, Ten Astor Place, New York, NY 10003.

A second organization, Writer's Guild of America (WGA), also has many agents as members. The Guild represents writers primarily for the purpose of collective bargaining in the motion picture, television, and radio industries. Agents as well as television, radio, and motion picture producers can become members of the WGA by signing the Guild's agreement on basic standards for the treatment of writers. Membership requirements include listing several professional credits accumulated within the preceding three years and an application fee of $2,500. The WGA has two offices, one in California and the other in New York. Agents and writers residing west of the Mississippi River should contact WGA, West, Inc. at 8955 Beverly Blvd., West Hollywood, CA 90048. Agents and writers east of the Mississippi River should contact WGA, East, Inc. at 555 West 57th Street, New York, NY 10019.

Although membership requires some degree of experience, joining one of these organizations will help improve your understanding of the profession and bring you more business. Many writers look at membership as a criterion in their search for an agent. A membership list and a brochure of other information are available from the AAR by sending $5 and a self-addressed, stamped (two First Class stamps) envelope. A membership list of the WGA can be obtained by sending them $2 and a self-addressed, stamped envelope.

CREATE YOUR OWN PROJECTS

You don't have to sit back and wait for authors to contact you—you can contact them. As an agent, you should be very familiar with the topics in which you specialize. You should also be familiar with what types of books are selling, which ones are selling the best, and any popular trends that are developing. Topics for new books can come from editors, clients, newspapers, magazines, television news programs, and talk shows. If you keep abreast of what is happening around you and in the publishing industry, you can create your own book projects and find suitable authors to write them.

Most established authors already have agents. Some successful authors even prefer not to use agents. It is unethical to try to entice a writer away from another agent; so how do you find competent writers who are looking for agents?

Many professions require good and even superior writing skills. Some examples would be English teachers/professors, journalists, editors, copywriters, freelance editors and writers, and educated professionals in other fields. People in these types of jobs would have skills necessary to write salable books. You can find these people in trade directories and association membership lists. The multi-volume directory, *Contemporary Authors*, for example, lists not only book authors but freelance writers and editors. You can also find writers in association membership lists and directories.

Most of these people will not have a book in progress, although some might. You could contact these people and offer to look at any projects on which they happen to be working. But many of them would probably try an agent of one of their writing friends—an agent the friend is satisfied with and recommends.

To get a qualified writer interested in working with you, what you can do is offer to give him a hot topic to write about and help him create the book and sell it to a publisher. As an agent, you should be familiar with the types of books that are selling and what subjects are hot. With this knowledge, you can formulate a book idea and approach a qualified writer to author it. Most writers would be flattered by your offer and, if they have the proper background and are not burdened with other responsibilities or commitments, would be enticed to accept your offer. Having a book published is a secret desire for all types of writers and editors. Presenting them with an opportunity to fulfill this dream will get you in association with skilled writers who may, not only do a good job on your proposed project, but remain faithful and productive clients for years to come.

Many different types of directories in your local public library can give you leads to qualified writers. *Literary Market Place* is one of the most useful resources in the book publishing industry. (See *International Literary Market Place* for resources outside North America.) It contains names and addresses of a wide variety of services and companies. You can find many competent writers under the literary services listing. Here you will find copyeditors, ghost writers, and others who could be candidates for your literary projects.

Another useful resource is *Gale Directory of Publications and Broadcast Media.* This annual directory contains names, addresses, and phone numbers of newspapers, magazines, and journals as well as radio stations, TV stations, and cable systems. This is one of your best sources for locating skilled editors and writers. It has a state-by-state listing and subject index for easy reference. Virtually all periodicals published in the country are listed. The larger publications, such as newspapers with circulations of 50,000 or more, include the names of editors of each department—the business editor, sports editor, foods editor, etc.

Say, for example, you had an idea of producing a biography of Steve Young, the quarterback for the San Francisco 49ers. One possible writer for the job would be the sports editor of the *San Francisco Chronicle.* You can look up the sports editor's name in *Gale Directory of Publications and Broadcast Media.* Once you have learned the editor's name, you might want to look him up in *Contemporary Authors.* If the editor is listed, you can read his biography and find out what books he has had published. If he has recently written several books, he probably already has an agent. If it has been many years since he has had a book published, or he doesn't have any book credits, or he is not even listed in the directory, he is probably not currently working with an agent and you could contact him with your idea. If the sports editor is unavailable or just too busy (as many journalists are) to take on the job, you might also consider contacting an assistant sports editor. Although assistant editors' names will not usually be listed in the directories, you can find out who they are by calling the publication or by looking at the bylines in a copy of the paper. Some other media directories include: *Syndicated Columnist Contacts*, *The Working Press of the Nation*, *Newsletters in Print*, and *The Standard Periodical Directory*. These are all similar to *Gale Directory of Publications and Broadcast Media*. You can also contact people who may be able to write a good nonfiction book even though they don't make their living with the written word. You can try knowledgeable professionals in numerous fields. What if you had an idea for a humorous book on public speaking? Although you may find some good writers in the directories listed above who could write such a book, it would take a bit of searching. A better directory to use is the *Encyclopedia of Associations*. This annual resource lists the names, addresses, contact persons, and descriptions of many thousands of organizations in North America. Here you can find information on the Public Speaking and Humor Club. By contacting this organization, you can find a person with just the experience you are looking for to write your book. Another directory of this nature is the *National Trade and Professional Associations of the United States*. See the Appendix for other resources, including those of international interest.

Chapter 6

HOW TO IDENTIFY MARKETABLE MANUSCRIPTS

Many well-written, marketable manuscripts are rejected for reasons which could be corrected. Knowing the reasons for rejection will help you in your search for salable material and will help your clients prepare their submissions properly. In this chapter you will learn why manuscripts are rejected, why editors are so choosy, and what you can do about it.

WHY MANUSCRIPTS ARE REJECTED

You have a manuscript you feel is worth publishing and perhaps even be a candidate for the bestseller list. You have faith in the work. But it is rejected by editor after editor.

If a book obviously has bestseller potential, why doesn't every editor jump at the chance to buy it? Can the professional judgment of so many editors be wrong? Not usually. Occasionally editors will pass by a masterfully written work simply because the subject material is new or different and the editors do not have experience with similar books to accurately compare it to. Therefore, it may be rejected. However, most manuscripts are rejected for a number of very good reasons. The following conditions describe the most common reasons why publishers reject manuscripts.

Improper Submission Format

One major reason for rejection is that the material is not properly prepared or is not submitted in the correct format. If the manuscript looks sloppy, is not double-spaced, or lacks slug lines, it will not be taken seriously. Publishers feel that if the author is not serious enough to take the time to prepare and submit the manuscript properly, it will probably not be well-researched or will be written in a careless manner. Many editors refuse to consider any material that is not submitted in the proper format. Or if a publisher requires that a query letter or book proposal be sent to him before receiving the manuscript, any manuscript sent first will automatically be rejected.

Some editors will consider submissions with slight deviations from standard format and submission procedures if the material shows promise. There are many resource materials available which explain how to prepare and submit manuscripts, including Chapter 8 in this book.

Lack of Writing Skills

Poor writing is another major reason manuscripts are rejected. Most novice writers simply do not write well enough to get published. I'm not talking just about mechanics, but about conveying thoughts and information in a manner that is instructive, easy-to-understand, and enjoyable to read.

At one time, editors could afford to spend time helping authors improve their writing skills and polish manuscripts. Nowadays, editors want material that requires very little editing. A manuscript may be on a topic the company is very much interested in and written by someone who has a great deal of knowledge of the subject; yet, if the author cannot adequately express himself, the material is of little value. It is easier to find another manuscript. An exception would be if the subject has a great deal of potential; then the editor may assign an experienced coauthor to help write the book.

Wrong Publisher

Submitting material to the wrong publisher is another common reason for manuscripts being rejected. Contrary to popular belief, publishers will not publish a book simply because it looks like a bestseller. Every publishing house has its own areas of specialization, with its own viewpoint or focus. Each publishes only those books that fit its personality and areas of specialization. Large publishing companies have a wide range of interests and publish many different types of books. These companies often have subsidiary publishing companies or imprints which specialize in certain types of books. For instance, Del Rey Books, an imprint of Ballantine Books, specializes in fantasy and science fiction novels.

Smaller publishing companies have fewer subject interests. Broadway Press, for example, is interested only in books on theater and performing arts. Backcountry Publications is interested only in outdoor recreation topics. If you send a potential bestselling romance novel to Better Homes and Gardens Books, or an entertaining children's picture book to Career Press, you will be rejected. Although these examples may be obvious, in most cases you cannot tell what types of books a company specializes in just by its name.

Many novice writers, not knowing any better, may simply look for addresses of publishers by thumbing through books lying around the house. Writers with a little more forethought will try to find books that are similar to the ones they have written, believing that the publisher will also be interested in their books as well. This is better than randomly sending out manuscripts, but there is a better way. Directories are available which list publishers and describe exactly what types of books they are looking for. (I will discuss this more in the next chapter.)

Limited Customer Interest

An author may produce a well-written book on a topic that is of interest to him. However, if there are not enough people willing to buy a book on that topic, the manuscript won't find a publisher. If the publisher cannot sell enough books to make a profit, he is not going to publish the book, no matter how good it is.

A book titled *The Yummy Liver Cookbook*, for instance, would have little appeal to most people and would not sell well in normal distribution channels.

Autobiographies from novice writers also fit this category. These authors are usually not famous, but average people who feel a need to tell their stories and express their thoughts on life. Unfortunately for them, this type of book will not sell. The average reader is not particularly interested in the day-to-day life of an auto mechanic or a stenographer. Unless you are a celebrity of some sort, most people will not be interested in reading your life story. Granted, there may be some exceptions for people who have led colorful lives, but their stories must be written with the skill of a professional writer to make them interesting and publishable.

Some books with limited customer interest could be profitable if produced and marketed by the right publisher. Even though a huge company like Prentice-Hall publishes some performing arts books, one on television camera operation is too narrow a subject for them. However, Players Press, which specializes in theater books, might be interested. Players Press has a market for this type of book because their distribution channels service theatrical markets.

Overworked Subject

The first few good books published on a new popular subject will always be the most successful. As more books on the subject are published, the competition for customers increases, adversely affecting the sales of all the books. After all, if a customer is interested in learning how to decorate cakes and buys a book on the subject, she is not likely to buy another one that covers the same material. If there are too many books already in print on a particular subject, a publisher will not be excited about publishing another. The competition is simply too great to take the risk.

It seems that once a book hits the bestseller list, everyone jumps on the bandwagon and writes copycat books. This often results in the writing and publication of mediocre books. Most copycat books do not match the original book's writing quality and content.

Most clones of popular books are not as successful as the original. In fact, I have seen books that are superior to bestsellers but do not do as well because they came out after the original. They do not get the reviews or have the prestige of being the original book on the subject. When faced with a choice between two books on the same subject, people will most likely choose the book that has had more publicity, which most likely will be the first book.

If the author and publisher are lucky, a book will be published just as a new trend or craze is becoming popular. These trends are very unpredictable. They may last only a few months or as long as several years. The books that become successful are the ones published as the trends are still growing in popularity. Once a trend has hit its peak and public interest starts to decline, publishers are not interested in producing new books on the subject. It takes nearly a year after a book has been accepted for publication before it is actually available for sale. A fad that was popular when the book was submitted for publication may be dead by the time it is published.

Most of what I have said here deals with nonfiction books, but the same is true for novels. Some subjects and plots are retold over and over again. Publishers always want something new and exciting, not a rehash of something already done.

Economics of Publishing

With the exception of university presses, most book publishers are in business to make money. The more books they sell, the more profit they make. Publishers are not particularly interested in works with great literary, academic, or social value. They want products that will sell, and sell well. Therefore, their primary aim is to find and publish material with the greatest sales potential. Most writers have little concept of what can be profitably published. Marketing is of secondary interest to them. They usually write on subjects that they are personally interested in, with little regard to its marketing potential, but publishers aren't going to throw their money around carelessly. They look for the books that they believe have the greatest chance of success.

Although publishers reject the vast majority of material they receive, not all of this material is unpublishable. They receive many good manuscripts that could possibly be profitable. But because most publishing companies operate on a narrow profit margin, they simply cannot publish every good book they receive. Consequently, book publishers must select those books which they feel have the greatest chance of making the most money.

Publishing is a blend of business sense and intuition that varies from one editor to the next. In deciding which books to accept for publication, book publishers rely on estimates of the books' sales potential and their editors' enthusiasm for the manuscript. If an editor likes the manuscript, she may convince her company to publish it. One editor may highly recommend a particular manuscript, while another editor may hate it. Personal preference often decides if a book gets published or not. However, a well-written and interesting manuscript is likely to find an enthusiastic editor to endorse it.

Editors are not always right. On rare occasions, they reject manuscripts that later become bestsellers. But as professionals familiar with book publishing, they do have an inside track on what types of books sell. And for the most part, they do a good job of picking out the best books for their companies. Simply because a book was rejected does not mean the editor did not like it or that it did not have sales potential. If the book did not conform to the publishing company's viewpoint or fit in with its list of books, it would be rejected regardless of its quality.

Overcoming Rejection

In summary, the reasons for rejection are: improper submission format, poor writing, submitting to the wrong publisher, selecting an overworked subject, limited customer interest, and economics. Except for economics, you and the author have almost total control over these conditions. Therefore, you can eliminate most reasons for rejection. Even with economics, you do have some control. If you have a well-written manuscript that would be of interest to many people, you will find enthusiastic editors who will want to buy it.

The unpublished writer commonly makes the mistakes discussed here. Published authors and authors represented by agents, in general, do not make these mistakes; that is why they are published. Their material is presented in a businesslike and professional manner and is therefore given more serious consideration.

One of the duties of agents is to help their clients prepare submissions properly and present them to publishers in a professional manner. Editors expect material from agents to be screened, and properly prepared and submitted. That is why many publishers prefer to work through agents rather than deal directly with authors.

WHY BOOK PUBLISHERS MUST BE SELECTIVE

Although the majority of the material publishers receive is unpublishable, they also receive a lot of well-written, publishable material. However, because of economic constraints, they cannot publish every good book they receive. The reasons for this are explained below.

Too Little Time

Editors, as a whole, are underpaid and overworked. Most of them must take work home daily just to keep from falling behind. In search of better working environments and the chance to get even a small raise, editors frequently jump from company to company. This is unfortunate for the authors and agents working with these editors, as new editors may lack the same enthusiasm for the author's work and even cancel books that were accepted by their predecessors.

Editors spend most of their time preparing books contracted for publication. This includes attending scheduling and sales meetings; writing jacket and catalog copy; composing sales information sheets; editing current projects; coordinating cover design, illustrations, and text; and dealing with authors (who can be demanding and troublesome, especially those of celebrity status). These duties eat up most of an eight-hour work day, leaving little time for reading and evaluating new manuscripts. For this reason, editors must focus their time on the most promising material that comes across their desks—material from successful authors they have worked with in the past, and agents who present themselves as professionals with marketable products.

Too Little Profit

Publishing is not as lucrative as you might believe. It's tough to make money in publishing. Many companies go out of business each year. In fact, some industries in this country spend more on just their advertising than the entire book industry earns in profit. Large advances paid to some authors for their books lead the public to believe that publishers can afford to pay huge sums of money. Not true. You only hear about these large advances because they are so rare, and only a few of the publishing giants can afford them.

Publishers give discounts to wholesalers, distributors, and book dealers which amount to an average of about 45 percent off the retail price. Prepress and manufacturing costs may account for 20 percent or more. Author royalties take out another 10 percent or so. Operating expenses (which include editors' salaries, marketing, administrative costs, and other overhead expenses) amount to about 20 percent. These are essential expenses that must be met, leaving about five percent for promotion, advertising, and profit. For the initial printing of a book, the publisher's profit amounts to only a small fraction the retail price.*

To make matters worse, most books are sold on a returnable basis. This means that if the books do not sell, the book dealer can return them for full credit. About 20 percent of all hardcover books and up to 50 percent of mass market paperbacks are eventually returned. Many of these books, damaged by shipping or shop wear, are unsalable or salable only at steep discounts. For mass market paperbacks, the store owners tear off and return only the covers, disposing of the rest of the book.

I know of no other industry where dealers can return unsold products to the manufacturer and, in some cases, even destroy them and get full credit. But this is what happens in the publishing industry.

Too Much Competition

Approximately one million books are currently in print and available for sale in this country. Every year over 147,000 new English-language books are published and distributed in the United States and Canada. Although this may sound encouraging to authors (more chances of getting published), it is really detrimental. With a million other books on the market, each new book must compete with them for the limited shelf space in stores, editorial space in the media, publisher's promotional dollars, and ultimately customers.

Competition can, and does, hurt the sale of many books. If, for instance, there was only one low-calorie cookbook in print, it would probably sell very well. If this book had to compete with 30 other books on the same subject, all things being equal, its sales would decrease by a factor of 30. From

---

* These figures are based on the first printing of a book. Reprints of successful books are cheaper to produce because prepress expenses are eliminated and press runs increased, making production more economical, so the profit margin would be slightly better.

a publishing standpoint this could make *all* of these cookbooks unprofitable.

An average-size bookstore may stock as many as 30,000-40,000 books. If you were a bookstore owner, which books would you choose? You have a million to choose from, and 147,000 new ones coming out each year. Like most store owners, you would choose those that have made the bestseller lists and those that have continually sold well over the years. Most of the books will be older books that have proven to be good sellers. Only a fraction of the space in bookstores is given to new titles. The huge majority of new books don't even see the inside of most bookstores. The obvious result is poor sales for many books which, consequently, go out of print. Most new books go out of print after the first printing.

Publishers know that new books are a risk, so they normally limit the number of books in the first printing to about 5,000-10,000 copies (these are *trade* hardcover books—books typically sold in bookstores, not little mass market paperbacks, directories, encyclopedias, professional works, or textbooks). Some companies' initial average print runs will be a little more, others a little less. You may hear of print runs significantly larger, but these are the exception and not the general rule. Larger print runs are reserved for those titles that the publisher feels confident will become bestsellers—those written by big name authors and film stars. The big publishing companies need to sell approximately 5,000-10,000 copies just to break even on the expenses of producing and marketing a new book. So, for most books the typical print run is limited to about 5,000-10,000 copies. If they can sell more than this amount within the first year, the book will probably make them a profit. If the book does not sell this initial printing after a year or so, it is usually considered a financial loss and is taken out of print. While a book that sells just over 5,000 copies may be a marginal success, a bestseller is one that sells upwards of 20,000 or more. To make the big-time bestseller lists, a book would need to sell several times that amount.

Too Many Failures

Here is an interesting fact that may surprise you: 80 percent of all new books will not be profitable enough to reprint. That's an 80 percent failure rate! This means that publishers make their profit on only 20 percent of the new books published. (Of course, this is in addition to reprints of books that have proven successful in previous years.) Of the 20 percent which are profitable, only a few could be considered bestsellers, and far fewer than that ever make the big-time bestseller lists. It's no wonder that publishing companies struggle financially.

The big publishing companies make their profits on relatively few titles. This means they must be highly selective in the books they choose to publish; they cannot publish every good manuscript they receive. The publisher must choose those books that have the greatest profit potential. If the publisher had to decide between two books, one of which is a literary masterpiece and the other is not, but has greater marketing potential, which one will he publish? The second one—the one that will make him the most money.

In Search of the Bestseller

For the reasons discussed above, publishers—particularly the big publishing companies—focus on publishing bestsellers (those that they believe will sell over 20,000 or 30,000 copies). Their survival depends on finding the next bestseller. This is a very important concept to understand because it affects what publishers will buy. They are not particularly interested in a good book with the potential to sell just a few thousand copies. They want blockbusters—books with mass appeal. They want books written by celebrities or about celebrities or other famous people. They want books that cater to new popular trends or that relate to current economic and political events, before public interest has reached its peak. They have a tendency to ignore new authors and concentrate on works from established writers who have already made names for themselves, books by literary superstars which will automatically be successful because these authors have built up reputations and faithful followings.

Publishers take a greater risk when dealing with an unknown author. They accept works by famous nonwriters, such as popular athletes, politicians, entertainers, and the like, but they may assign a competent coauthor to do the majority of the writing. If your client's material doesn't fit into these categories, it will be difficult for you to sell it to the large publishing houses.

KNOW WHAT SELLS

To be a successful agent, you must have a sense of what can and cannot sell and who to sell it to. You must know what types of books are marketable and can make money for a publisher. After all, publishers are in business to make money, not create literary masterpieces or feed starving authors. They publish only those books they believe will make them the most profit.

To fully understand market conditions and keep abreast of what is currently popular, you should specialize in select areas. Do not try to be too generalized or you lose effectiveness as an agent. Choose areas to focus on and learn as much as you can about them. Learn which companies publish books in those areas. Learn editors' names. Many agents, in their course of business, develop a first-name association with editors. These editors become familiar with the agents and learn to trust them. Consequently, they give serious consideration to material received from them.

Know your markets. Choose subjects you enjoy reading. If you don't care for westerns, you would not be a good judge of that type of book. You may choose as many subjects or categories as you feel you can adequately master, but attempting to market any and all types of books will reduce your effectiveness. Also, authors should be leery of agents who will represent any book. Such agents are considered either amateurs or con artists. An inexperienced agent may accept any type of book from children's picture books to adult romance novels just to build up a clientele, but this is not recommended.

Check the bestseller lists on a regular basis. The lists published in *The New York Times Book Review,* while not scientifically accurateare, the national indicators of how well books (hard and soft cover) are selling. Each week the New York Times calls key stores across the country to ask what books have been selling best that week. If a bookstore has a large stock of Danielle Steel novels in stock, that's what they're selling or trying to sell, and that's what they report. Books by big-name authors automatically get more attention because those are the books bookstores stock and push. Just being listed on the bestseller list actually increases a book's sales. Therefore, high-profile books by popular authors are often listed even though actual sales initially don't warrant the listing. The bestseller lists are helpful guides, but keep in mind that they are not totally accurate.

Read good books in your area of specialization so that you have a measure by which to judge manuscripts. Keep up continually with what new books are published in these areas and which ones become popular sellers and which ones don't. Request catalogs from publishers and study them (see Chapter 7 for information on getting addresses). Visit bookstores and see what books are stocked, and which ones are selling. Although bookstores may try various new books, they will only restock the best selling titles.

Become familiar with *Books in Print.* This directory lists all books sold in the United States and Canada which are currently in print. You can look up subjects, authors, or titles in one of several volumes. Using the number of books listed on a particular subject, you can determine its popularity and get ideas for developing your own book projects. You would also use *Books in Print* to check the potential competition from new nonfiction books. If a client's book is similar to others already in print, publishers will not be enthusiastic about publishing another one.

Learn everything you can about the world of publishing. Read books on writing and getting published. Subscribe to writers' magazines such as *Writer's Digest* and *The Writer,* two of the most popular periodicals of this type. (See the Appendix for additional resources.) Another magazine which would be of great benefit to you is *Publishers Weekly*. This magazine is devoted to book trade news. It contains articles about editors, agents, publishers, and what they have sold and bought, as well as information on new books and trends in the publishing industry. This is your best source for keeping abreast of what's happening in publishing.

Chapter 7

THE MARKETS

As you learned in the previous chapter, you don't want to send manuscripts to just any publisher. Doing that is a waste of time and money. Without direction you could spend your lifetime trying to find the right one. In this chapter, I will show you how to locate the proper markets for your books.

Most novice writers have no idea how to sell their books to publishers. They don't even know how to find publishers to contact, let alone publishers who would have an interest in the type of book they have written. Often, beginning writers will simply get publishers' addresses out of published books and hope for the best. Needless to say, this is an ineffective approach. One of the benefits of working with an agent is that agents know where to find interested publishers. This information is not hidden, but readily available to anyone. Names, addresses, and interests of publishers can be found in publishing directories.

There are several different directories available which list book and magazine publishers, as well as many other services and businesses associated with the publishing industry. In these directories you will find the names and addresses of publishers, as well as learn about the types of material they publish. This information will help you locate the right publisher for your client's works. As a literary agent, you should become very familiar with these resources and use the valuable information they contain.

WRITER'S MARKET

The most valuable publisher directory for writers and agents is *Writer's Market*. It is your guide to the book publishers in the United States and Canada, including many international companies which have offices in several countries. It doesn't list all publishers, only the ones who are interested in receiving submissions. In it you can find information on over 4,000 publishers (800 book publishers, 3,200 magazine publishers), their names, addresses, and descriptions of the types of material they publish. It tells you where to sell articles, books, fillers, greeting cards, novels, plays, scripts, and short stories. All knowledgeable writers and literary agents use it as their primary marketing reference. Because there are so many changes in the publishing industry—new companies start up, others go out of business, names and addresses change—this book is updated and a new edition is published every year.

In searching for a publisher you should refer to *Writer's Market*. Don't send your manuscript until you have referred to this directory first. One of the primary reasons manuscripts are rejected is that the subject material is not appropriate for that publisher. All publishers receive manuscripts on subjects in which they have no interest. If the senders had referred to *Writer's Market* first, they wouldn't have wasted their time and money. No matter how good a book may be, editors will not be interested unless it fits their publishing program.

Besides describing the types of books and articles they publish, *Writer's Market* also provides the publishers' most current addresses, editors' names, the number of books published each year, the type of submissions they want, the time they require to evaluate submissions, and more. All of this information is important to you if you want to make a sale.

At the back of the *Writer's Market* book section is a subject index. If your manuscript is about dogs, you would turn to the index and look under the heading of "Animals" for publishers who publish books on animals. You then look these publishers up in the Book Publishers section, which is in alphabetical order. No matter what the subject of your manuscript, by using the subject index you can locate publishers likely to be interested. This will save you from thumbing through each of the 800 listings.

Most publishers listed will send you a copy of their writer's guidelines if you send them a SASE. These guidelines contain the most current and detailed information concerning the type of material they publish, and explain how they want to receive submissions. Some guidelines are very specific, while others are more generalized. Many will specify how to prepare manuscripts. One publisher may want the manuscript set up one way, while another may request it in a completely different format. In Chapter 8, I will show you the commonly accepted format for manuscripts. However, you may find publishers who will request something slightly different. If they don't specify, use the examples as described in this book.

LITERARY MARKET PLACE

Another important directory you should become familiar with is *Literary Market Place*. It contains a comprehensive listing of nearly 2,000 pages of publishers, book producers (packagers), editorial services, literary agents, marketing and publicity firms, book manufacturers, distributors, trade associations, photographers, translators, consultants, illustrators, trade publications, workshops, and almost any other kind of service or company involved in the book publishing trade. Many of these services can be invaluable in getting your client's work prepared for publication.

Literary Market Place is updated and published annually. It lists about 3,700 publishers, and includes a Small Press section. Book publishers are required to publish an average of at least three new books per year to be included in the main Book Publishers section. Publishers who do not meet this requirement may be listed in the Small Press section for a fee.

Unlike *Writer's Market*, the publishers listed in *Literary Market Place* include both those who actively look for and buy material from writers and those who do not. Some companies are not included in *Writer's Market* because they specifically asked not to be listed. The reasons are that they receive too many unsolicited submissions or they do not accept any unagented submissions.

The entries in *Literary Market Place* generally include name, address, phone number, key personnel, brief description of types of books published, number of titles printed in previous year, total number currently in print, and year founded. It contains a more detailed listing of key personnel than *Writer's Market*, but the description of the types of books published and what each publisher is looking for is not as comprehensive.

The main publisher listings are in alphabetical order. Following this are geographic (state-by-state), type (scholarly, trade, mass market paperback, hardcover, etc.), and subject indexes. The Canadian book publishers section follows.

Literary Market Place is a large and expensive book (priced at about $160). For this reason, it is best that you go to your library to use it. It is usually shelved in the reference section of the library and probably cannot be checked out, so you must use it in the library.

Another book you may be interested in, which is very similar to *Literary Market Place* and published by the same company, is *International Literary Market Place*. It contains the same type of information as *Literary Market Place* for companies and services outside the United States and Canada.

OTHER DIRECTORIES

There are many other publisher directories available, some of which may be more appropriate to your needs than either *Writer's Market* or *Literary Market Place*.

Writer's Market contains information of interest to writers of various materials, including books of all types, magazine and trade journal articles, greeting cards, plays, etc. *Literary Market Place* is of primary interest to those dealing with books. The publishers of *Writer's Market* also produce a series of references aimed at more specific markets. If you're interested in selling poetry, for example, you can look in *Poet's Market*. Other reference books include *Children's Writer's & Illustrator's Market, Children's Media Market Place, Religious Writer's Marketplace, Novel and Short Story Writer's Market, Scriptwriters Market*, and *Humor and Cartoon Markets,* among others. These books are all laid out in a format similar to *Writer's Market* and include both book and periodical publishers.

An excellent comprehensive directory of small publishing companies is the *International Directory of Little Magazines and Small Presses*. This reference contains both very small publishers and self-publishers, as well as moderate-sized companies. Listings of book publishers include the year founded, the number of books published each year, and the number of books each publisher currently has in print, which gives a good idea of the company's size and stability. Magazines are also included.

Both American and Canadian publishers are listed in most of the directories mentioned above. Some directories are devoted entirely to Canadian publishers. They are *Canadian Publishers Directory, The Book Trade in Canada/L'Industrie du Livre au Canada, The Canadian Writer's Guide*, and *The Canadian Writer's Market*. The two primary sources for both foreign and domestic companies are *International Writer's and Artist's Yearbook* and *Directory of Book Publishing*. The latter reference is compiled by the British Publishers Association and the Federation of European Publishers, and contains an extensive listing of major publishers (as well as agents, distributors, marketing services, etc.) in Europe and the Commonwealth countries.

LARGE PUBLISHING HOUSES

The largest commercial publishing houses are usually the agent's prime markets. The size of a publishing company is based on the number of new books it publishes each year. Large publishing companies produce in excess of 100 new books a year. Some crank out as many as 600 or more. There are several hundred commercial book publishers, but only a few dozen can be considered large. Although relatively few in number, they produce the majority of the trade books published annually.

The large companies are the ones who have the most money to buy books, have the best sales network, the largest advertising and promotional budgets, and the most experienced staffs. They are usually better able to publicize and sell books than smaller publishers. They also have the finances to pay six-figure advances. For these reasons it is to the advantage of agents with general interest books to approach the publishing giants first.

If the big companies show no interest, then approach the mid-sized companies. If the medium and large publishers don't buy your material, you might consider some of the alternate markets discussed below. In fact, for many special interest books, your client's chances of publication are better with an alternative market and may even produce greater profits.

SMALL AND INDEPENDENT PRESSES

Independent or small presses are companies that publish fewer than twenty or so new books each year, although some companies which publish as many as 30 books a year may also call themselves small presses. These companies can be little Mom-and Pop-operations or modest-sized corporations with several dozen employees.

Although small presses don't publish as many books as large companies do, they are more numerous. One-third of the publishing companies in operation today started less than ten years ago. Most of these would be considered small presses.

The smaller publishing companies are much more receptive to new authors and agents. They receive fewer submissions than large publishers and aren't as discriminating about material that doesn't exactly fit the formal submission format. They are more willing to work with an author who needs a little help polishing a manuscript, thus turning a work that might have been rejected elsewhere into a published book.

Even though small presses will be more receptive to books with limited customer appeal and will give new authors a chance, they are not pushovers. In general, they publish quality books equal in construction and content to those of the large companies. A poorly-written manuscript will not be published by a small press any more than by a big company. Small presses expect authors and agents to show respect and send a professional submission; they are just as intolerant of sloppy or careless work as a large publisher.

The big publishers prefer that new writers hone their skills by working with smaller presses before approaching them. So, the small presses provide a service to budding writers who need experience. Very few writers ever sell their first book. It usually takes several years before a writer develops the skill to be able to sell his or her writing consistently. Most first sales are to small companies.

Most small presses specialize in only a few subjects. Many concentrate on a single topic which may be very broad, like health and fitness, or more defined, like antique doll collecting. They become experts in their fields of publication. They know what can sell and to whom they can sell it. In fact, sometimes they can do a much better job selling books in their specialty than the big publishers can, even though they have fewer resources and less financial and promotional muscle. They have a keener sense of the market, and are willing to spend the time promoting books that large publishers could not sell as effectively.

High Text, for example, is a small company which publishes books dealing with electronics and related subjects. They reprinted two books that were originally published by McGraw-Hill and Prentice Hall—two of the industry's largest companies. One of the books was on integrated circuit applications and the other was on shortwave radio listening. The original publishers sold the books only through their normal retail book channels. After mediocre sales, both books were taken out of print. When High Text reprinted the books, they largely ignored the traditional book markets and focused their efforts on electronics parts dealers, shortwave radio distributors, and mail order catalogs for radio and electronics enthusiasts. In less than one year, High Text was able to sell more copies of both books than McGraw-Hill and Prentice Hall had in over three years! Because of their flexibility, aggressiveness, and marketing knowledge, small publishing companies can be more successful with books within their speciality.

A question you might ask is: if big companies have more money to spend on advertising and promotion, can't they advertise their books to bring people into the bookstores? Experience has shown that most types of advertising for books is not cost-effective. Advertising is not directed toward persuading the public to rush down to their nearest bookstore to buy some new book, because this doesn't work. Most advertising is directed to book buyers to inform them that a new book by a favorite author or celebrity is available.

Publishers focus on other promotional methods to publicize their books: book reviews, author signings, and talk show appearances, to name a few. Other than a few select titles, no book gets the promotion it deserves. The truth is that large publishers will spend very little time or money promoting most of their books. The largest part of their advertising and publicity dollars goes toward promoting a handful of their most promising bestsellers. The rest of their books get little more exposure than being mentioned in their general catalog.

Production and overhead expenses must be taken out of the publisher's revenues first. This leaves little for advertising and profit. With limited capital available, publishers channel most of their advertising dollars into actively promoting only a small number of their books. They can't promote every book as they should because doing so would eat into their already narrow profit margin.

With a small publishing company, overhead expenses are smaller and other expenses are carefully monitored to prevent waste. This gives the small publisher a larger profit margin and allows him to give each book individual attention and some degree of promotion and publicity. Even though smaller companies may not spend much on advertising, the money they do spend is targeted to the most receptive markets. They invest much more time and effort promoting each of their books than a big company would, simply because each book has a greater bearing on the company's overall success.

Because these companies are small, they are more likely to be adversely influenced by economic conditions. They could go out of business at any time. Large companies could too, but they are usually a bit more stable.

With some caution, you can greatly reduce the chances of working with a company that will unexpectedly go bankrupt. First, choose companies that produce at least three new titles each year. Companies that produce fewer than this are probably too small to be of much benefit to you. They have limited resources, shallow marketing networks, and are highly susceptible to economic conditions. Choose a strong company, which can be determined by the number of new books they publish each year and by the length of time they have been in business. If the company has been around for 10 years, they apparently know what they are doing and have an established marketing network. Be very cautious with any small press that has been in existence less than three years. Information on the number of books published, length of time in business, as well as many other important aspects of the company can be found in *Writer's Market* and other directories.

Another disadvantage of small presses is that they are less able to take advantage of the sale of subsidiary rights. A large hardcover publisher has more contacts and influence, so is better able to exploit subsidiary rights.

The primary disadvantage with small presses is that they generally offer smaller advances. Some don't offer advances at all. There is nothing wrong with this. An advance is always a payment against royalties, that is, money paid to the author before the book has earned any. It is not extra income paid in addition to the royalties. It is part of the royalties that the book is expected to earn. Small companies may offer only a few hundred dollars, if anything at all.

Most books do not sell as well as the author, agent, or publisher had hoped. Advances are usually non-refundable. So, if a book does not sell well enough to compensate the publisher for the author's advance, the publisher suffers the loss. The author and the agent come out ahead by receiving a larger royalty payment than the sales of the book warranted. Since most books (80 percent) published by the big publishers are not reprinted, agents try to get the biggest advance possible. They know that, in many cases, the advance will be bigger than the amount the book will actually earn. This is an important part of contract negotiations.

Because their success ratio is much greater than 20 percent, small presses aren't affected as much by books that don't sell well. It may take twice as long to sell some of their more general interest books as compared to a larger publisher, but they keep the books in print and reprint them over and over again. But some books do go out of print, and it is almost impossible to predict which ones will. So, an agent is usually better off getting his client as big an advance as possible, regardless who publishes the book.

It is important to keep in mind, particularly when working with small publishers, the types of books they publish. Small publishers are successful because they specialize in only a few subject areas. They can even be more effective selling books in these areas than the publishing giants because they know the market better. For this reason, many large publishers have imprints which specialize, so that they can have the small company "feel", yet benefit from the marketing capabilities of a large company.

For general interest books, a large company will probably sell more books than a small press can. But small presses generally keep their books in print much longer, with the possibility of selling more books over the long run. For specialized subjects, small presses are frequently much more successful than the big publishers.

UNIVERSITY PRESSES

Another market which you might consider is the university press. There are approximately a hundred university presses in the United States alone. Most of their funding is subsidized by the government, private foundations, and other groups. Although, if funding is not available from these sources, the author may be asked to make a financial contribution.

Contrary to what many people may think, university presses do not publish just textbooks and class manuals. In fact, they leave most of that up to textbook publishers. University presses publish a wide range of topics of both general and specialized interest. Topics include history, biography, politics, education, religion, science, business, economics, geography, poetry, and fiction, to mention just a few. Most have a strong interest in regional titles. Some of their titles are very academic, while others are similar to any other popular book that may be found in the bookstore.

University presses, more than other publishers, will consider publishing material simply because of its literary quality and value. Unlike commercial publishers, the university presses' main goal is not to make a profit or to find bestsellers. They are not focused on finding books with mass appeal or big sales potential. University presses consider, on merit, almost any subject of scholarly interest. They look for evidence of original research, use of reliable sources, clarity of organization, and complete development of the theme with documentation and supportive footnotes or bibliography. They want books that will make significant contributions to knowledge in the fields treated.

If they think a book has merit, it has a chance of being published. Sometimes, if the book appears to have limited marketing potential and outside funding is not available, the publisher will offer to produce a limited number of the books under a subsidy arrangement with the author. This means the author would be expected to pay part or all of the printing cost. Although university presses are not focused toward making huge profits, they do need to pay expenses. Developing, producing, and selling books costs money. Usually the author, on a subsidy arrangement, will pay some portion of the cost to get the book published. Since huge sales are not expected, the print run will be small and the cost to the author relatively low. The amount could vary anywhere from a few hundred to a couple of thousand dollars.

University presses are respected in the book industry and produce top-quality products. Their books are sold to all book outlets including bookstores, libraries, schools, department stores, and elsewhere.

Writer's Market lists university presses in its main book section, along with most other commercial publishers. Because money is not the focal point of their publishing program, they offer low advances, if any at all. The average print run for their books is typically 1,000 to 2,000 copies. Most of their books (95-99 percent) are submitted by the author without the aid of an agent.

You won't make much money with university presses, but they are very receptive to new authors because the work is judged on its merits, not its marketing potential. If you can't interest a commercial publisher in your client's work, you may interest a university press. Publication by a university press will give your client's career a boost and give him a valuable publishing reference for the future. Most new authors dream of getting on the bestseller list, but if that is not possible, they are thrilled just to get published and see their names in print. A university press could accomplish this.

SUBSIDY PUBLISHERS

Many publishers besides the university presses subsidize their publishing. Some of these companies are almost indistinguishable from commercial publishers. Others operate entirely as subsidy presses and are distinctly different in operation and purpose from the publishers discussed so far in this book.

Commercial publishing companies involved in subsidy publishing get their funds from private and government organizations and foundations just like university presses, as well as from the authors. These presses, like university presses, feel an obligation to produce quality or scholarly works even though the financial rewards may not be great. When an author is asked to share in the cost of producing his or her book, it is often termed co-publishing. Companies involved in co-publishing are primarily commercial publishers. Their subsidy programs comprise no more than 50 percent of their publishing program and usually much less.

A publisher may offer to co-publish a book with an author if the book fits his line but has a limited market. For example, a publisher who has a strong line of pet books may ask a writer to share in the production costs for a book on a rare breed of dog. The publisher will actively market the book along with all of his other books and pay the author a typical royalty of 5-15 percent. Sometimes the publisher may request that the royalties start after 1,000 or 2,000 books have sold, to compensate him for his expenses. This could be instead of the author's subsidy or in addition to it. The amount charged for co-publication is typically $2,000-$5,000. If you have a specialized book with a limited market or can't get a client's book published otherwise, co-publishing is a legitimate option to consider. Like university presses, co-publication provides an opportunity for authors to get their works published by a respectable company.

There are other publishers whose publishing programs consist almost entirely of author-subsidized books. These commercial subsidy presses are often referred to as "vanity" presses because they satisfy the author's need of seeing his or her book in print, and such books get little or no respect anywhere in the book industry. Vanity presses are distinctly different from the publishers who are involved in co-publishing as previously described. They make their profit on the money they charge authors and not on sales. In fact, almost all books published by vanity presses end up as financial failures for the author. It is a waste of time for an agent to approach these publishers.

FOREIGN MARKETS

You are not limited to only the publishing companies in this country. You can approach publishers and agents in other countries. Many of them may be more suitable for one of your books than a domestic press. A spy novel set in Quebec may be of greater interest to a Canadian publisher than one in the United States. A book about Sumo wrestling might be of greatest interest to a Japanese press.

The United States produces more books than any other country. American books are found all over the world, in both English and non-English speaking countries. Two-thirds of the books sold in Canada, for example, come from the United States. Competition with American publishing companies is so strong that most Canadian publishers focus on books with Canadian content. If you were to seek a Canadian publisher, your chances would be greater if your book's subject was Canadian oriented. The same is true for many other English language publishers, some of which are located in countries where English is not the dominant language.

The greatest markets for most English language manuscripts are English speaking countries, but many other countries where English is commonly spoken also sell and publish English language books.

Some of your manuscripts could be translated into another language by foreign publishers. If a company has editorial offices or distribution in North America, a book may be produced in more than one language. Most foreign publishers do not have American offices. If the publisher doesn't, he may only be interested in obtaining the publishing rights in his native tongue. A publisher in Chile may only be interested in the Spanish language rights, which means he has sole right to publish and distribute the book in Spanish language countries.

You can find foreign publishers listed in *Directory of Book Publishing* (2 volumes), *International Literary Market Place*, *Writer's and Artist's Yearbook*, and *International Directory of Little Magazines and Small Presses*. The first three references also list foreign literary agents. Working with a foreign agent will give you the best chance of finding a suitable publisher.

If you want to contact foreign publishers directly, you should first get a copy of each publisher's author guidelines. The guidelines explain more fully what each publisher wants and how he wants submissions prepared. In foreign markets, the requirements can vary greatly.

Because of the expense of sending mail out of the country and the difficulty of working directly with a foreign publisher, most agents work with subagents in the foreign country. Books that may be of interest to a foreign audience are sent to agents in that country. If those agents like the manuscript, they will work with you to sell the material. The commission is usually shared between the two agents.

Chapter 8

SUBMISSIONS

The author prepares all submission materials except for the cover or query letter, which will be written by the agent. All initial submissions include a query letter. In some cases, the entire submission is simply a query letter; in other cases, the query may accompany sample chapters, a book proposal, or the entire manuscript. What is sent on the initial contact with the publisher depends on the company's submissions policy, as outlined in their listing in *Writer's Market*.

QUERY LETTERS

A query letter is a brief but detailed business letter written to interest an editor in the manuscript. Almost all initial submissions require a query letter in one form or another. Most editors want to see a query before being sent the manuscript.

Sending a query letter first is actually best for both you and the editor. The editor isn't burdened with a multitude of unwanted manuscripts, and you save on postage and time.

An editor is much more willing to read a one- or two-page letter than a 300-page manuscript. Also, she has a much easier decision to make. You are not asking her to make a purchase—you are merely asking her to take a look at your material. If she responds positively to your letter, she will be prepared for it when it comes; it will not be an unsolicited submission. And since she requested it, she now owes you a personal response. *This requires her to actually read your material.* This way, your submission will get into the hands of the right person and be given a fair evaluation. If, however, you send the manuscript first, you might only get a form rejection letter and you will never really know if anyone actually looked at it.

Appearance

When you send a query letter, you are, in essence, sending a sales letter to a business in an attempt to sell a product—your client's writing. The query must be set up in a businesslike format. You should have stationery printed with your name, agency name, address, and phone number.

The query letter should be typed (single-spaced) on white paper and limited to one or two pages in length. Handwritten letters show a lack of professionalism. If you use a computer, use a letter-quality printer. If you are using a typewriter and make a mistake, do not cross out the error and retype it or use correction fluid—retype the letter. Neatness does make an impression.

On the first page of the letter, you should type the name of the editor you are submitting it to, the company name, and address. This information is found in trade directories like *Writer's Market.* Most business letters use a block-style format. Separate each paragraph with a space without indenting. Address, salutation, body of letter, and closing are all left-justified. Page 107 shows an example.

The query must be written in an interesting and compelling style, free of spelling and grammatical errors. Don't try to be cute or funny; just give the facts. Don't waste the editor's time by giving your opinion of how good the manuscript is or predicting that it will be a bestseller. Making such claims only makes you look naive and amateurish.

Address

Submissions addressed to the "Fiction Editor," "Submissions Editor," "Editorial Director," or some other title usually wind up in the slush pile or are automatically returned. To avoid the initial round of rejections, you should address the letter to an editor by name. Editors are a highly mobile group and frequently move from one company to another or change positions within a single company. Even though the publishing directories are updated every year, as many as 25 percent of the listings in the current editions may already be outdated. Some big publishing companies will return a submission unread if it is addressed to an editor who is no longer there. To avoid this problem, you may want to call the company first and ask to whom you should send your query. This is more important with large companies than it is with the smaller ones. The editors at smaller companies are much more stable.

A letter addressed to a specific person unquestionably receives more attention than one that is not. After all, if the sender knows the editor by name, the editor may have had previous dealings with the agent or may even have requested the submission, so it will receive preferential treatment.

As you make contacts with editors, you will get to know them and they you. Addressing your submissions to a specific editor who is familiar with you will keep your material out of the slush pile. If editors have received worthwhile material from you in the past, they will be anxious to see your new submissions. Of course, the opposite is also true. If all you ever send them is garbage, they will show little interest in your submissions.

When approaching a publisher you have not worked with previously, the best person to contact is an associate or assistant editor. These are junior editors who are anxious to establish relationships with agents who can help build their careers. They are still trying to prove themselves and are eager to work with new agents and writers. Since most of the projects they receive are given to them by higher-ups, they will be flattered that you sent material directly to them. In response, they will treat your submission with more respect. The names listed in *Writer's Market* and other directories usually are those of executives who pass most submissions on to the editorial staff for evaluation. Get the name of the associate or assistant editor by calling and asking. Because there will be several editors and assistants, you will want to get the name of the person who would be most interested in your type of manuscript. So, state that you want the submissions editor who considers science fiction, romance, cookbooks, or whatever your topic happens to be.

In the salutation of the letter, use Mr. or Ms., not the editor's first name. If gender cannot be determined, use the full name (e.g., Dear Leslie Jones). Once you have corresponded for a while, you may begin your salutation with the editor's first name, but usually only after the editor begins calling you by your first name.

Content

The content of the query letter should be brief and to the point. It should convey a positive, professional attitude and avoid sounding like a used-car salesman. Busy editors appreciate a direct approach void of worthless sales hype.

Your opening paragraph should briefly describe the subject of the book, so that the editor knows which category it belongs to and what the manuscript is about. You may mention that your book is in the same category as a particular, well-known book. However, don't say that your manuscript is as good as, or better than, this book. Let the editor decide that on her own.

Here is an example of a simple, direct opening for a novel:

> I represent a client who has just completed a 50,000-word science fiction novel entitled <u>Artificial Intelligence</u>. It is about an untested electronic brain that is transplanted into the skull of an accident victim.

This paragraph furnishes the editor all the introductory information she needs to get an idea of the book and its category, and to make an initial judgment about the work. No wasted words. No ravings about the merits or potential sales figures. Just straight forward information.

If necessary, you may describe the contents of the book in greater detail. If the book is fiction, briefly describe the storyline and characters, and include the conflict. Keep it short. Give enough information about your story to spark the editor's interest.

You can also mention any special training or experience that qualifies the author to write the book. This would include education, work experience, publishing credits, and any awards or special recognition your client has received.

Closing

In the closing of your letter, make a direct request to the editor for permission to send a proposal or the complete manuscript. The request is important because you are asking the editor to take action and give you a favorable response. This is a positive, motivating technique used in advertising. Don't end your letter by just saying "Thank you for your time..." or "The completed manuscript is available if you would care to see it..." or "If you are interested, please let me know..." or some similar closing. Be positive. A better ending would be "I'm looking forward to your timely response" or "May I send the complete manuscript to you?" An ending like this indicates that you expect a response and the editor will feel more obligated to give you one.

If the manuscript is not yet completed, you may specify the completion date and approximate length. Also indicate if you are sending query letters to other publishers.

Enclose a self-addressed, stamped, return envelope. Use a #10 business-sized envelope. The editor will use this to send you a reply. If you don't include a return envelope, you will hear from the editor only if she is interested in seeing your work.

If not, she will simply trash your letter without sending a response.

For a detailed look at writing query letters, I recommend reading *How to Write Irresistible Query Letters* by Lisa Collier Cool. This book is geared more for authors than agents, but it contains many interesting examples and ideas.

MULTIPLE SUBMISSIONS

To save time and increase your chances for a positive response, you may contact several editors at the same time. This is referred to as a simultaneous or multiple submission. In the past, the standard practice was for an author to send submissions to one publisher at a time. It took each publisher a month or two to evaluate the material and respond. Authors and agents could reach only a few publishers a year. Since some manuscripts could be rejected by 20 or 30 publishers before being published, it could takes years to find the right publisher. So, nowadays it is generally acceptable to send out multiple submissions.

If you are sending out several query letters, let the editors know that you are making a simultaneous query. Although simultaneous submissions are acceptable to most publishers, some do not like them and will not consider any material submitted this way. Their reason is that they don't like the hassle of competing with other publishers. Check the individual listings in *Writer's Market* for those publishers who do not accept simultaneous submissions.

If two or more publishers do respond favorably to a simultaneous query and eventually offer to buy your manuscript, you have the opportunity of choosing one. You may select the one you feel will benefit you and the author the most. If the publishers liked the material well enough, you may even get them competing with each other. However, it is rare for publishers to want to invest much in a work from a new author, so they probably will not negotiate much.

Never use a form letter as a query, even if you are sending out multiple submissions. Although you may say the same thing in each letter, put the appropriate editor's name and address on each letter and sign it. Photocopied letters are unbusinesslike and almost always rejected.

BOOK PROPOSALS

A book proposal is some combination of a cover letter, introduction, a synopsis, an outline, and sample chapters. The exact combination of these will depend on the publisher, as indicated in *Writer's Market*. The cover letter is written by the agent, but the rest of the proposal is usually prepared by the author.

There is no one correct way to prepare a book proposal. Some proposals may be very simple and consist of only a cover letter and a few sample chapters, while others may include a table of contents, detailed introduction, market analysis, author bio, extensive outline, and several chapters, amounting to nearly a hundred pages.

New authors often do not know how to prepare proposals properly, so the agent must give them guidance. The book proposal is a formal presentation of the manuscript. It is a tool used to interest editors in the book and, in many cases, even sell it.

For seasoned writers who have many writing credits, a detailed proposal is important because the publisher will often purchase the book after reading only the proposal. This is particularly true for nonfiction. These authors have built up a record of successful books, and the editor can feel confident that the new book will be written competently. New and relatively inexperienced writers, on the other hand, are usually required to submit their entire manuscript before a decision is made to buy it. Editors take a greater risk with newer authors who don't have a proven track record. For new authors, the book proposal is a tool used to interest editors in reading the manuscript.

Cover Letter

You will always send a cover letter along with the author's book proposal. If the book proposal is your *initial* contact with the editor, the cover letter acts as a query letter. It should be written by the agent and contain the same information as a query letter.

If you sent the editor a query letter first and she requested a proposal, the cover letter should not be a repeat of your query letter nor used to make a sales pitch. Keep it to only a paragraph or two and just briefly remind the editor that she requested the material.

An example of a query letter that would accompany a book proposal is shown on the following page.

Introduction to the Proposal

Some *nonfiction* book proposals may include an introduction which would contain much of the same information mentioned in the query letter, but in more detail. You would use an introduction if this information cannot be adequately covered in a two-page query letter. An introduction isn't necessary for most novels because all the information the editor needs to know can be stated in a short cover letter.

The introduction consists of an overview of the project, describing the scope and content of the book, including information on promotion, marketing, and competition. If the author has extensive professional qualifications or writing credits, that information would also be included.

If you include an introduction to your proposal, you can reduce your cover letter to basically the opening and closing statements as described in the section on query letters. Do not staple or bind your proposal. Label the top of each page with your name, an abbreviated book title, and page number.

WHITE LITERARY AGENCY
483 First Street
Santa Barbara, CA 93140
(916) 444-1234

Linda Smith
Big Books Press
1417 Broadway
New York, NY 10020

Dear Ms. Smith:

I represent William Snyder, who has just written a 60,000-word manuscript entitled How to Write Great Ads. This book teaches the skill of writing effective advertising for print ads, direct mail packages, and radio and television commercials.

The book demystifies advertising writing, using a step-by-step process and workbook format. It breaks down the ad writing process into a series of simple steps. Included are fill-in exercises and other self-tests for practicing each step immediately after learning it. This book gets would-be ad writers up and running quickly, creating effective ad pieces, and feeling confident.

Enclosed, you will find a chapter-by-chapter outline of the book and three sample chapters.

There are only three other books currently in print on ad copywriting— all of which were written over ten years ago and are essentially outdated. Snyder's book incorporates the newest trends and developments in this field, including the latest statistics and marketing studies.

Mr. Snyder has a degree in Communications from Harvard University. For the past fifteen years, he has worked as an advertising copywriter and presently is Vice-President of Classic Advertising Agency in Los Angeles. He has been teaching copywriting for the University of Southern California Continuing Education Department for six years. He was the recipient of the 1994 California Copywriter's Association's "Copywriter of the Year" award.

May I send you a copy of William Snyder's manuscript, How to Write Great Ads? This is a simultaneous submission. I look forward to your reply.

Yours truly,
Paula White

Example of a query letter.

Synopsis

Publishers usually request either a synopsis or an outline as part of the proposal. They both serve a similar purpose. Often, the terms are used interchangeably and what you send to the publisher depends on the type of manuscript you have and whether or not it is complete. Basically, a synopsis is a brief description of the book, while an outline is longer and more detailed. Both the synopsis and the outline should be typed in manuscript form, as described later in this chapter.

A synopsis is used primarily when you have a completed manuscript ready to send to the editor. It is a brief, descriptive summary of the book, limited to just a few, double-spaced pages. Its purpose is to interest the editor in the manuscript enough to request to see it (thus avoiding the unsolicited manuscript barrier).

The synopsis should be interesting and easy to read. It not only describes the book, but also gives the editor a sample of the author's writing style and ability. If the synopsis does not flow smoothly or contains spelling, grammar, and punctuation errors, the editor knows the manuscript will be the same and show no interest. Have the author reread and rewrite the synopsis as many times as necessary until it is as good as he can possibly make it. Don't ruin your chances of a sale by submitting a hastily-written synopsis.

Outline

While the purpose of the synopsis is to convince the editor to *read* your manuscript, the purpose of the outline is to convince the editor to *buy* your manuscript. The editor may buy your client's idea and commission him to complete the manuscript, or she may request to see the completed manuscript before she makes an offer. Whether or not the manuscript is complete, you can send an outline.

The outline covers the plot or highlights of your book chapter-by-chapter and is much more detailed than the synopsis. Each chapter of the outline may consist of only a few paragraphs or cover two or more double-spaced pages. If the outline is for a novel, it should include all major characters, the main plot, subplots, and any pertinent details, including revealing the ending. A completed outline may consist of 20 or more pages. Detailed outlines are normally used for uncompleted manuscripts. Most published authors sell their books by way of a book proposal containing a comprehensive outline before they have finished writing the manuscript. Some sell it after having written only a couple of preliminary chapters.

A thorough outline shows the editor that the author has thought about and researched the subject adequately and can complete the manuscript successfully. Editors want to avoid accepting a manuscript idea that has only a few completed chapters with an outline of several additional chapters, only to discover that the author couldn't find much more to say, resulting in a skimpy, 84-page book. Editors also wish to avoid having the second half of the book turn into a philosophical platform inappropriate to the rest of the book. A detailed outline helps eliminate these and other problems. If it is a novel, the editor also wants to see if the author can fully develop the story and maintain the reader's interest.

The completed manuscript does not have to follow the proposed outline exactly. Editors realize that as the book is being written, new ideas will emerge or concepts may need to be separated or combined. Often, editor's suggestions will also lead to changes.

Often, particularly with medium and large-sized publishing houses, an in-house editor must convince superiors to buy the book. A well-written outline will help. The senior editors, who will probably never read the book, will make their decisions based, in part, on the junior editor's enthusiasm and the outline.

If a publisher wants the proposal or outline formatted in a certain way, he will indicate this in his author's guidelines. Guidelines are free for the asking, if you send a self-addressed, stamped, business envelope.

Sample Chapters

Most publishers prefer to see sample chapters before

requesting the entire manuscript. You should send two to three chapters unless specified otherwise in *Writer's Market*. Some publishers indicate they want certain chapters, while others leave that decision up to the author or agent. The publisher may require the first three chapters so that he can see how the author develops the book. Another may want the first, a middle, and the last chapter to see how it begins, progresses, and ends. Most publishers let the author choose the chapters to send. The material should total between 40 and 60 pages. You need to send a sample large enough to demonstrate the author's writing skill.

MANUSCRIPT PREPARATION

Editors at large publishing houses may receive hundreds of manuscripts every month. These manuscripts come in an assortment of styles and formats. Some follow the guidelines for proper manuscript preparation, many do not. Either consciously or subconsciously, the appearance of each manuscript affects the editor's attitude toward it.

Editors judge a work by the way it looks even before they read it. Some editors will reject a manuscript without reading it simply because it is messy or was not typed in the proper format. A manuscript should never be rejected for this reason. It is a very simple matter to type and present a manuscript properly.

Although the appearance and structure of a manuscript says a lot about the author, slight variations in the format are perfectly acceptable. There is no *one* correct way to prepare a manuscript. A publisher will not reject a manuscript simply because an extra space is inserted below the title. Publishers are not that picky. Professional writers use somewhat different formats, but their manuscripts all contain the needed information and are easy to read.

A manuscript that doesn't follow the proper format signals to the editor that the writer is an amateur, lacks knowledge of the publishing and writing profession, and is too lazy to learn how to do it properly. This suggests the writing in the manuscript will be second-rate.

One of the responsibilities of literary agents is to help clients present their work in a professional manner.

Professional Appearance

Editors' time is precious. They like material that is easy to read. For this reason, handwritten manuscripts are totally unacceptable. Dot-matrix computer printouts are usually undesirable and many editors won't accept them unless they are of letter-quality. Submissions should be prepared using a good typewriter, word processor, or computer that can produce letter-quality characters. Laser printers do an excellent job and although not necessary, they do give a good impression.

Do not submit material created on old, worn-out typewriters that blur the letters or have uneven lines and spacings. Errors crossed out with XXs are unacceptable, as are too many corrections made by hand with a pen. A few errors can be corrected with correction tape or fluids. If there are too many errors, have the page retyped.

A great manuscript will go unread if the type style is not easy to read. Avoid using all capital letters, cursive, or any other fancy type style. With computers and laser printers, it is tempting to use fancy fonts. The easier the manuscript is to read, the better your chances of getting it read. Use a standard type style for all of your submission materials.

Use good quality, 20-pound bond, 8.5 x 11-inch, white paper for the manuscript, typed on only one side. All the margins on the page should be at least 1 to 1.25 inches. Sheets should not be stapled together. A paper clip may be used to hold them together, if you desire.

If it is printed from a computer on fanfold paper with tractor edges, tear off the feeder strips and separate the pages before you send them. Make sure the characters are clear and dark enough to be read easily.

Some publishers accept electronic submissions (on disk).

However, do not send a disk unless you inquire with the editor first.

Title Page

A title page is used for book-length manuscripts. This page contains important information about your client and the work. Information on this page should be single-spaced.

In the upper left corner, type the author's name (use his real name, not a pseudonym), mailing address, and daytime phone number.

In the upper right hand corner of the first page, indicate the approximate number of words in the manuscript. This is important because publishers have a wordage range they must work within.

You may also put a copyright notice under the word count, if you wish. This is done by typing the word "copyright" or showing the symbol "©" followed by the year and the author's name. A handwritten copyright symbol is acceptable. The copyright notice is optional.

The title should be placed one-third of the way down the page. It should be centered and in all capital letters. The word "by" should be typed two spaces below the title and the author's name or pseudonym two spaces below that. The line with the author's name is referred to as the *byline*.

The agent's name, address, and phone number are typed on the lower right side of the title page. Page 114 shows an example of a title page for a book-length manuscript.

The Text

Begin each chapter on a new page. The chapter title should be placed about one-third of the page down from the top. Type the chapter number, double-space, and the chapter title in all capital letters. Drop down two double-spaces and begin the body of your manuscript. See the example on page 115.

Headers and Footers

Since the manuscript is not stapled or permanently bound

together, each page must be identified. The author's name and the page number are entered on a single line on every page after the first. This is called the *slug line*. The slug line keeps pages in order, and prevents them from accidently being mixed with someone else's material and getting lost. Do not number the title page or include it in the total page count.

The slug line can be placed near any of the four corners of the page. If it is placed at the top of the page, it is called a "header" and if it is placed at the bottom of the page, it is called a "footer". The most common place for the slug line is at the upper left corner of the page (see the examples on pages 115 and 116).

The slug line can take a couple of different forms. What's important is that essential information be included—author's name and page number. A shortened form of the title may also be added. The page number can come immediately after the name or be positioned toward the far right side of the page. The book title, chapter title, or chapter number can be typed on this line or beneath it, if desired.

If the author is using a pseudonym, his real name is typed first, followed by his pen name in parentheses and the page number. For example, Smith (Schultz) - 2. Two double spaces should separate the slug line and the text.

Begin each chapter on a new page and include a slug line with the page number.

Front and Back Matter

Front matter and back matter are parts of books, but not part of the main text. Front matter includes the table of contents, dedication, acknowledgements, preface, list of illustrations or tables, and foreword. Back matter includes the appendix, bibliography, glossary, list of abbreviations, and index. Not all of these are needed or contained in every book or manuscript. The index, for example, is almost always compiled after the manuscript has been set up in book form. Novels do not normally need a table of contents, foreword, list of tables, etc. A table of contents should, however, be added to nonfiction manuscripts.

Karen Smith
P.O. Box 1222
New York, NY 10012
(212) 223-4321

96,400 words

JAMAICA SHORES

by

Karen Smith

Star Literary Agency
938 South Street
Chico, CA 97823
(916)456-5839

The title page for a book-length manuscript.

CHAPTER 1
THE ADVENTURE BEGINS

I was born in the year 1632, in the city of York, of a good family. My father earned a good estate by merchandise in London, and leaving off his trade, retired to York; from whence he had married my mother.

I had two elder brothers, one of whom was a lieutenant-colonel who was killed in the battle near Dunkirk against the Spaniards. What became of my second brother I never knew, any more than my father or mother knew what became of me.

Being the third son of the family, and not bred to any trade, my head began to be filled very early with rambling thoughts. My father, who was very ancient, had given me a competent share of learning, as far as house education and a country free school generally go, and designed me for the law. But I would be satisfied with nothing but going to sea; and my inclination to this led me so strongly against the will, nay, the commands of my father, and against all the entreaties and persuasions of my mother and other friends, that there seemed to be something fatal in

The first page after the title page of a book-length manuscript. Page numbering starts on this page.

Jamaica Shores/Smith   312

In the meantime, I in part settled myself here. For, first of all, I married and had three children, two sons and one daughter. But my wife dying, and my nephew coming home with good success from a voyage to Spain, my inclination to go abroad and his importunity prevailed, and I engaged to go in his ship as a private trader to the East Indies. In this voyage, I visited my new colony in the island, saw my successors, the Spaniards; had the whole story of their coming to, and adventures in, the island after my departure. All these things, with some very surprising incidents in some new adventures of my own for ten years more, I may, perhaps, give a further account hereafter.

The End

The last manuscript page of a novel.

Page numbers are not normally needed on front matter, as they are usually compiled after the rest of the manuscript. But page numbers can be put on the back matter. A slug line with title and author is always included. All front and back matter are prepared in basically the same manner. The slug line is typed about a inch below the top of the page (for a header). The chapter title, typed in all capital letters, is entered at about a third of the way from the top of the page. The text begins two double-spaces below that.

Ending
For fiction, the words "The End" are centered and placed three double-spaces after the last sentence of the manuscript. If it is nonfiction, "###" or the symbol "- 30 -" is used, which signifies the same thing.

MAILING SUBMISSIONS

There is more to sending submissions than just putting them in the mail. If you do it the wrong way, you will be perceived as an amateur and will get the same treatment that most novice writers receive.

Envelopes and Postage
When sending an editor a manuscript, use an envelope that is large and strong enough to hold it. Use at least 9 x 12-inch envelopes or even a box.

Make sure you use the correct postage. Packages received with the stamp, "Postage Due", are usually sent back to the senders unopened.

If you want a response from the publisher, you must include a self-addressed, stamped envelope (SASE). Whether you are sending a one-page query letter or a full manuscript, you need to include a return envelope with postage. Some editors will not respond even if you do send a SASE, simply because they are burdened with so many submissions. Most, however, will send you a reply if you have included a SASE. Even if you do not send a SASE, editors will respond if they are interested in seeing your material.

Send an envelope large enough to accommodate the material you want returned, preaddressed, with stamps in place. If you are sending your material in a #10 envelope, send a business-size return envelope, folded in thirds. You could also use a slightly smaller #9 envelope, which will fit into the #10 envelope without folding. If you are submitting material requiring a larger envelope, include an envelope large and sturdy enough to hold it. A 9 x 12-inch envelope or mailer can be folded in half.

You may decide that you don't need to have the manuscript returned. However, you still want to receive a response from the editor. If all you want is a response, all you need to send is a business-size SASE. The manuscript, if not accepted, is then discarded. In your cover letter you may indicate that the manuscript need not be returned.

If you write to any publisher or agent outside the country, you cannot use your country's postage stamps on your return envelopes. Stamps on the return envelope must be from the country from which it is to be mailed. A Canadian publisher, for example, must have Canadian stamps, which are difficult to find outside of Canada. What you can do is include an International Reply Coupon (IRC) with your envelope. You can purchase IRCs at any post office. The publisher exchanges them for postage at his post office. Postage rates are different in foreign countries, so make sure you buy enough IRCs for the return.

Since postage out of the country can be very expensive, especially for heavy manuscripts, it is best to send only a return envelope and IRC and let the publisher keep the manuscript.

If an editor requests a book proposal or the completed manuscript, mark on the outside of the envelope, "Requested Proposal" or "Requested Manuscript." This way the editor and staff know that it isn't just another unsolicited submission and should not be thrown into the slush pile. You should also use mailing labels with your company name printed on them. This way, editors will know the package was sent in by an agency and will give it preferential treatment.

Manuscripts can be sent in various ways. Overnight delivery is the quickest, but is usually unnecessary. First Class mail (or Priority mail for packages over 12 ounces) or UPS ground service is suitable for most purposes. If you don't mind waiting a couple of extra weeks, you can send them by Fourth Class mail. Books and manuscripts can be sent Fourth Class at a substantially cheaper rate. The savings may be only a few dollars per mailing, but if you send manuscripts to a lot of publishers, the cost will quickly add up. If you use Fourth Class, print "Return Postage Guaranteed" under your address to ensure that your package will be returned to you if it is undeliverable.

You might also consider using Certified or Registered mail if you are sending important documents, photos, tapes, or anything of value. Certified mail requires the receiver to sign for it on its arrival. This provides you proof of delivery. Registered mail goes a step further by requiring a signature from every post office it passes through so it can be traced if need be. Naturally, these services cost you extra.

You could insure the contents of your package if you like, but this insurance is payable only on the tangible value of the material being sent. A manuscript could be insured only for the cost of the paper. So, unless you are sending something of value with the manuscript, it is best not to bother with insurance.

You may want to include photos with the manuscript or book proposal. To prevent undue damage, reinforce your mailing envelope with cardboard inserts. Write on the outside of the envelope, "PHOTOS—DO NOT BEND." You may also use a heavy cardboard envelope, available at packaging or photography supply stores.

Always keep a copy of the manuscript, illustrations, and any documents. Once this material leaves your possession, you have no control over what happens to it. It may be lost or destroyed in the mail, misplaced by an editor, or accidentally thrown out by a member of the office staff.

Record-Keeping

Keep track of all queries, proposals, or manuscripts that you send. Don't just sit back and wait for a response. Record what was sent (e.g., query, proposal, manuscript), date sent, who it was sent to (including editor's name and phone number), and enclosures (e.g., photos, documents). You should also find out the response time listed in *Writer's Market* and record that date. Mail can be, and too frequently is, lost en route to its destination. In such cases, you can wait forever without receiving a response. To reduce this problem, some agents include a self-addressed, stamped postcard in addition to the return envelope with the submission. On receipt of the materials, the editor is asked to return the postcard. This way, the agent knows that the editor actually received the submission.

On every self-addressed reply card or envelope you should put the return address of the publishing company. The reason for this is that not all editors will put their company name on the card. Also, companies change names or go through restructuring that alters their names, thus you may get a response with a different name on it or no name at all. If you write the company name on the envelope or card, you will know who sent it. If the company did change names, you can update your records.

When you receive a response, record the result and the date. This record is important. You may send out 40 or more packages before finding a publisher who will buy your material. Many books go through numerous rejections before finally being published, so don't give up!

Your record shows who has received your material, who is interested, and who is not. You can't expect to keep all of this information in your head. Clients want to know what's happening with their books. You need to be able to show your clients what progress you have been making. You might consider sending them copies of the publishers' responses to show them that you are diligently working to sell their books. If your clients never hear anything from you except that all the responses are negative, they have no proof you have actually done anything.

If you're working with a new client, it is important to demonstrate to him you are doing everything in your power to sell his book.

Follow-Up

If you sent a SASE, most publishers will send you a reply. If you have not received a response after the stated time has passed, write a follow-up letter politely inquiring about the status of the material. Address your follow-up letter to the same person to whom you submitted your material. If you used only the editor's title, without the name, your chances of a response are less likely. Your follow-up letter may say something like the following:

> On January 14th of this year, I submitted a manuscript from my client, Bonnie Freeman entitled The Clover Leaf Club for your consideration. It has been two months since the manuscript was sent, and I have not heard back from you. Would you please let me know what its status is at this time?
>
> I have enclosed a self-addressed, stamped envelope for your convenience. I look forward to your timely reply.

Unless you know the editor personally, don't call her on the phone! One thing busy editors can't stand is being annoyed by pesky agents or authors. Just send a reminder. You certainly don't want to annoy the editor. She may discard your material just because she doesn't want to deal with you.

To make it easier for the editor to give you a reply, you may send a self-addressed, stamped postcard. On the back of the card, say something like this:

> On January 14th of this year, I submitted a manuscript from my client, Bonnie Freeman, entitled The Clover Leaf Club for your consideration. It has been two months since the manuscript was sent and I have not heard back from you. Would you please

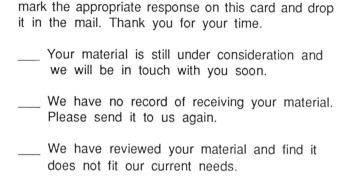

mark the appropriate response on this card and drop it in the mail. Thank you for your time.

___ Your material is still under consideration and we will be in touch with you soon.

___ We have no record of receiving your material. Please send it to us again.

___ We have reviewed your material and find it does not fit our current needs.

Don't forget to put the name of the editor, company, and address in the return address corner of the card.

Record the date of your second letter and wait a few weeks. If you still don't receive a response, you may write another letter of inquiry. Be polite and courteous. If the editor doesn't respond to your letter in a few weeks, chances are she is not interested in your material and will not reply. A phone call will probably do little good and may be screened by a secretary anyway. Some editors won't respond to any submission from an unfamiliar agent unless they are interested in the material, even if it does contain a SASE. In that case, repeated inquires or phone calls won't do any good.

Any editor, however, who requests to see your manuscript owes you a response. You should keep in contact with her until you receive one.

ADDITIONAL INFORMATION

This chapter explained how to prepare and submit book proposals and manuscripts. There are many books in print that describe this process in more detail. I highly recommend that you read as many of these as you can, so that you gain a firm understanding of the submission process. See the Appendix for a list of recommended sources.

For an in-depth treatment of how to write a book proposal, two books I recommend reading are *How to Write a Book Proposal* by Michael Larsen and *Write the Perfect Book Proposal* by Jeff Herman and Deborah Adams. These books explain how to create a professional-looking book proposal that will get editors' attention. These are good resources to recommend to authors you work with who need a little help preparing quality proposals.

For a more in-depth look at manuscript preparation, I recommend you get a copy of the book, *Guide to Manuscript Formats* by Dian Dincin Buchman and Seli Groves. This comprehensive resource not only discusses book formats, but covers television scripts, teleplays, television sitcoms, soap operas, audio-visual scripts, screenplays, and plays. The latter information is particularly important to agents dealing with the theater and film industry.

AUTHOR-AGENT AGREEMENTS _____

While it is possible for an agent to represent an author without signing a contract, it is best to have some form of written agreement. A contract protects both the agent and the author. It clarifies the important aspects of the relationship, thus avoiding possible misunderstandings and disputes later on. Terms of representation can be made with a formal contract or with a more casual letter of agreement. Both serve the same purpose and say basically the same things.

The letter of agreement is a letter written by the agent, outlining important terms and conditions of representation. Unlike a formal contract filled with legal terminology, which may be confusing, the letter of agreement is often written in more understandable English. The client signs it, makes a photocopy, and returns the original letter to the agent.

Some letters of agreement are more formal than others, ranging from modified contracts to friendly letters. Many agents prefer to use a letter of agreement because it suggests that the agent's involvement will be personal and friendly. A contract, on the other hand, projects a more businesslike relationship and, because it is more detailed, it also leaves less room for misunderstandings.

Although most author-agent agreements are similar, none are exactly alike. Pages 126 to 129 illustrate a sample contract. Terms and conditions can be modified or added, as the agent or author see fit.

EXPLANATION OF CONTRACT

If you have not had much experience reading contracts, you might at first be apprehensive, but they really are not that difficult to understand if you have them explained to you. For this reason, we will go over the contract illustrated on the following pages clause by clause.

Agency
Paragraph one states the geographical area where the agent is authorized to represent the author. The agent usually is authorized to represent the author worldwide, but in some cases may be restricted to a single country. The works the agent is authorized to market are identified. Usually, if the author has more than one manuscript, the agent will market them all. The rights which the agent shall market are also indicated. In some cases, the author may want to reserve some rights. For example, magazine editors frequently buy first serial rights to portions of books before they are published, or second serial rights after publication. These book excerpts are published as magazine articles. An author familiar with selling magazine articles may want to retain these rights in order to market them personally.

Best Efforts
The agent promises to devote sufficient time and energy toward marketing the author's work. A lazy agent can be useless to the author. Without this clause the author is obligated to stay with the agent until the contract is terminated. This provision

AGREEMENT, entered into as of this___day of ____19___, between _____(Agent's Name)_____ (hereinafter referred to as the "Agent"), and _____(Author's name)_____ (hereinafter referred to as the "Author") located at_____(Author's Address)_____, his or her heirs, executors, administrators, successors and assigns: Concerning book(s) or manuscripts(s) presently titled: (hereinafter referred to as the "Work")

NOW, THEREFORE, in consideration of the mutual covenants herein contained, the parties agree as follows:

1. Agency. The Author appoints the Agent to act as his or her representative:
(A) in the following geographical area_____(worldwide)____
(B) Agent shall market all of Author's literary rights, primary and subsidiary, including but not limited to publishing, motion picture, stage, and television rights, in all the literary material which Author submits to Agent during the term of the agency, and the pre-existing literary material listed above. Any rights not granted to the Agent are reserved to the Author.

2. Best Efforts. The Agent agrees to use his or her best efforts in submitting the Author's work for the purpose of securing assignments for the Author.

3. Subagents. Agent may appoint others to assist in fulfilling this Agreement, including subagents.

4. Samples. The Author shall provide the Agent with such samples of work as are from time to time necessary for the purpose of securing assignments. These samples shall remain the property of the Author and be returned on termination of this Agreement.

Sample author-agent agreement.

5. Author's Approval. Agent agrees to submit to Author all offers received. No agreement shall bind Author without Author's written consent.

6. Collections. Agent agrees to collect and receive for Author all monies due from marketing Author's literary rights, to hold that money safely while it is in Agent's possession and control, and to remit to Author within fifteen (15) days after Agent receives it.

7. Commissions. Agent shall be entitled to retain as Agent's full agency commission, 15% of all monies collected from the sale of the Work, except:

(A) If Agent appoints a subagent to sell subsidiary rights, the combined commission for all such co-agents shall not exceed 20%.

(B) Whenever foreign taxes are deducted at the source of monies due, Agent's commission shall be based on the balance after said tax deduction.

8. Expenses. Agent shall be entitled to deduct and retain from such monies the full amount of direct out-of-pocket expenses such as, but not limited to, copyright fees, manuscript preparation, telephone calls, and postage. Agent shall obtain approval from Author before incurring any expenses over fifty dollars ($50). Agent may deduct travel expenses Agent incurs on Author's behalf only if Author approves them in advance.

9. Records. Agent shall maintain accurate books and records of Author's account, and shall submit complete and accurate statements to Author semiannually. Author shall have the right to inspect and audit (or have Author's accountant inspect and audit) those books, during normal business hours and after giving Agent reasonable written notice. Such inspection shall be at Author's own expense, but if the audit uncovers an error in Author's favor greater than 10%, Agent will bear the expense.

10. Term. This Agreement shall have an initial term of one (1) year, beginning on the date of the signing of this Agreement. The Agreement shall renew automatically for additional terms of one (1) year unless terminated by thirty (30) days' prior written notice by either party to the other.

In the event of the bankruptcy or insolvency of the Agent, this Agreement shall also terminate. The rights and obligations under paragraphs 4, 6, 7, and 9 shall survive termination, provided that in the event of termination the Author shall have the right to have payments (less commissions) paid directly to the Author rather than to the Agent as set forth in Paragraph 6.

If, within sixty (60) days after the date of termination, Author, or an agent representing Author, enters into a contract for the sale of literary rights with respect to which Agent had been negotiating before the termination, and the terms obtained in the contract are no more favorable than the terms which Agent had obtained, then that contract shall be deemed entered into during the term of this Agreement.

11. Arbitration. Any disputes arising under this Agreement between the Agent and the Author shall be referred to the arbitration of two persons (one to be named by each party) familiar with book publishing or their mutually agreed umpire, in accordance with the Rules of the American Arbitration Association; judgment on the award rendered may be entered in any court having jurisdiction thereof. The arbitrator may award reasonable attorney's fees to the prevailing party.

12. Right to Contract. Both Agent and Author represent

and warrant that they are free to enter into and fully perform this Agreement and that they do not have nor shall have any contract or obligations which conflict with any of its provisions.

13. Independent Contractor Status. Both parties agree that the Agent is acting as an independent contractor. This Agreement is not an employment agreement, nor does it constitute a joint venture or partnership between the Author and Agent.

14. Amendments and Merger. This Agreement represents the entire contract made by the parties. Its terms cannot be modified except by a written document signed by the parties.

15. Governing Law. This Agreement shall be governed by the laws of the State of _____.

IN WITNESS WHEREOF, the parties have signed this Agreement as of the date set forth above.

Author_____   Agent_____

guarantees that the agent will put forth an honest effort to sell the author's work.

Subagents

The agent is given permission to use others to help market the author's work. Agents outside the agency may be used to help sell subsidiary rights. Examples would be selling British Commonwealth rights through a literary agent in England or movie rights through an experienced script agent.

Samples

The author is responsible for preparing book proposals, sample chapters, and copies of the manuscript for distribution by the agent. The agent may send these materials or make copies to send to publishers. The agent may charge the cost of reproducing some of these materials to the author.

Author's Approval

The author is given the right to examine and approve or disapprove all publishing offers that the agent receives.

Collections

Payments from publishers will be sent directly to the agent, who will deduct his commission and deliver the rest to the author within 15 days.

Commissions

The agent's commission is specified. In this example, it is 15 percent. If the agent uses one or more subagents to sell subsidiary rights, the commission will be no more than 20 percent, each agent receiving a share. In some countries, taxes are deducted from royalty payments, so the agent's commission is based on the after-tax amount.

Expenses

Expenses the agent incurs in marketing can be handled in any number of ways. Some agents do not charge clients for incidental office expenses directly related to marketing the author's work, such as postage, telephone calls, and photocopying, but do charge for overnight delivery, overseas communications, and necessary travel expenses. Larger expenses in which reimbursement is expected should always be approved by the author beforehand. Some agents bill clients or deduct all of their expenses from their royalty payments (as is the case in this example). Others may simply charge a one-time fee to cover all expected incidental expenses.

Records

The agent is obligated to maintain accurate records of royalty payments and expenses charged to the author. The author has the right to have an accountant examine the agent's records for accuracy. This clause is important to the author because it allows him access to the agent's records, making sure the agent is dealing ethically.

Term

The length of the contract is given as one year. After that time the contract can be terminated by either the author or agent with a written notice. It may take the agent a full year to market a manuscript adequately, especially if it requires additional editing or rewriting and if it is not easily sold. Once an agent has offered a manuscript to all appropriate publishers without receiving a positive response, he can do little else. The client may be dissatisfied and may believe the agent didn't try hard enough. At this point, if the author feels another agent would have more success, he is free to try.

If the agency goes out of business, the contract is automatically canceled and the author is free to seek another agent. If a manuscript is sold to a publishing house and the author-agent agreement is terminated, the agent is entitled to receive commissions for that book as long as that publisher keeps it in print. If the agreement is terminated, the author can have his share of the royalty payments sent directly to him, rather than going through the agent.

If the author rejects a publishing offer while the contract is in force and then, after the contract is terminated (within 60 days), sells the work to the publisher at terms no more favorable than those which the agent obtained, the agent is entitled to the full rights of representation.

Arbitration

Disputes between the agent and author can be settled in a court of law. The party that wins the case will have all attorney's fees and costs paid by the losing party.

Right to Contract

Both parties guarantee that they are legally free to enter into this agreement and will not have other obligations that prevent them from performing as agreed upon.

Independent Contractor Status

This clause states that the agent is acting as an independent contractor and not as an employee or partner of the author. The reason this paragraph is added is because an employee could claim employee benefits; a partner could claim an equal share; an independent contractor can claim only the comissions and expenses specified. This put into the Agreement for the author's benefit.

Amendments and Merger

This contract represents the entire terms of the agreement between author and agent. Verbal agreements are not part of the contract and are not legally binding. Terms and conditions not mentioned in this contract can be added only by a written document signed by both parties.

Governing Law

Disputes between the author and agent will be settled by a court of law in the state designated by the agent. This is usually the state where the agent conducts business.

Chapter 10

PUBLISHING AGREEMENTS

All trade book publishing contracts are similar and contain similar provisions. If you have a good understanding of one representative contract, you can generally understand most publishing agreements. Each publisher has a basic printed contract, known as the *boilerplate*. These are standard contracts that vary somewhat from house to house. They contain blank spaces for information and terms which vary from author to author, for example, the author's name and address, as well as the amount of the advance and royalty rates. When editors talk about their "standard contract," they are referring to the boilerplate without any changes. Although publishing agreements protect both the publisher and author, they always favor the publisher, as would be expected. All agents fight to change the publisher's boilerplate, in order to make the contracts more balanced.

If you have never worked with a publishing agreement before, it may seem like a mass of legal clauses and terms which are foreign and intimidating. However, if you take the time to read a contract and accompanying explanation, as provided in this chapter, you will find that they are not as intimidating as

21. ASSIGNMENT
This Agreement shall be binding upon the heirs, executors, administrators, successors, or assigns of the Author, and the succes- sher, but no assignment by operation of law or by the shall be made without the

15. TERMINATION
If the Work goes out of print in all United States editions and if the Publisher fails to reprint, or to cause a licensee to reprint, a United States edition within six months after receipt of written notice from the Author, unless prevented from doing so by circumstances

ONTRACT
Author, or his or her agent, iod of two months from the Publisher retains the right to delivery of the signed r.

Agree- granted ll revert to third e under Author's he Work lable in ublisher ation of ns after

have signed this Agreement

_____ Date_____

uthor's Birth Date_____

_____ Date_____

true, would constitute a breach of any of the foregoing warranties (hereinafter collectively referred to as "Claims") and any liabilities, losses, expenses (including attorney's fees), or damages in conse- quence thereof.
(c) Either party shall give prompt written notice to the other party of any Claims.

11. COPYRIGHT
(a) The Publisher agrees to copyright the Work in the Author's name and to secure its rights and the author's rights under the U.S. Copyright Act. The Publisher is authorized, but not obligated, to take steps to secure copyrights in other countries in the Territory.
(b) If the Publisher supplies at the Publisher's expense or illustrative material for the Work, such material may be separately as the Publisher shall deem appropriate.
(c) If during the existence of this Agreement the co be infringed or a claim for unfair competition shall ari unauthorized use of the Work or any part the the format thereof or the characters or situation if the parties proceed jointly, the expenses and be shared equally, and if they do not proceed have the right to prosecute such action, and s expenses thereof, and any recoveries shall t such party shall not hold the record title of t party hereby consents that the action be brou
The Publisher shall n to take such legal s

nd or suit val of the

have the s of this d above.

license

and exclusively, to exercise, to dispose of or to license the disposition of the following subsidiary rights and shall receive 50 percent of the proceeds thereof:

made hereunder prior to such reversion as liquidated damages for the publisher's failure to publish the Work.

6. AUTHOR'S COPIES
The Publisher shall give to the Author 10 free copies of each edition of the Work published by the Publisher. The Author shall be nt of 40 percent wn use, but not n these author's

ion
ook
ling
ign
ers
to
ket

12. WARRANTY
(a) The Author sole owner of the W nature whatsoever in into this Agreement Publisher; the Work

(f) If the Author fails to deliver the Work within the time specified, or if the author delivers the Work and it is not satisfactory to the Publisher, the Publisher shall have the option to terminate this agreement; in which case the Publisher shall not be required to publish the Work and the Author shall repay on demand to the Publisher any guaranteed advance or any other sums theretofore paid to the Author. Upon such termination and repayment, all rights granted to the

advance against yalties, the sum signed contract ot.

or
her
to:
im-

AGREEMENT made this _____ day of _____ 19___, between_____ whose address is _____(hereinafter referred to as the "Author"), and _____ (hereinafter referred to as the "Publisher") concerning a work tentatively titled_____ (hereinafter referred to as the "Work").
WHEREBY, in consideration of the mutual covenants herein contained, the Author and Publisher agree to the following:

1. GRANT OF RIGHTS
The Author hereby grants and assigns to the Publisher and his assignee(s) and/or licensee(s) the exclusive right to publish, sell, and distribute the Work in book form, for the full term of copyright and any renewals and extensions thereof, throughout the world (hereinafter referred to as the "Territory").

2. THE MANUSCRIPT
(a) The author agrees to deliver to the Publisher not later than_____, two typewritten or computer generated copies of the complete manuscript of the Work in the English language, approxi- mately _____ words in length, in content and form satisfactory to the Publisher. If the manuscript for the Work is not satisfactory, the Publisher may request the Author to make changes or revisions. If the Publisher requests changes and revisions, the Author shall make them within such time as the publisher may reasonably request and resubmit the manuscript to the Publisher.
(b) The Author shall deliver written authorizations for the use of any materials owned by a third party included in the manuscript. Any fees for such permission shall be paid by the Author.
(c) The Author shall provide all drawings, maps, charts, photo- graphs and other illustrative material which publisher deems necessary for the Work. If the Author fails to do so, the Publisher shall have the right to prepare or cause to be prepared any illustrative materials and charge the cost thereof to the Author.
(d) If in the Publisher's opinion an index, bibliography, foreword, introduction, or preface for the Work is necessary, the Publisher will so inform the Author. If these materials are not prepared by the Author, the Publisher shall have the right to prepare them and charge the cost therefor to the Author's account.
(e) The Publisher shall have the right to edit the Work for the original printing and for any reprinting, provided the meaning of the text is not materially altered, and shall have the right to publish and promote the Work in suitable style as to paper, printing, binding, cover and/or jacket design and to fix or alter title and price.

with a galley proof of the nd return all proof sheets Author agrees to pay all cost of composition for s of printers' errors) which alter the type has been returned by the Author. the Author. If the Author fied above, the Publisher approval of the proof.

shall be the Author's next ke to write another book uscript for the Work has

shall not print or publish, rtion of this Work, or any matter that might compete ered by this agreement.

Work, within 24 months of its own expense; if the e Author, by fire or water pliers or any other causes Publisher may cancel this r deems necessary. If the ublished, the Work within ne thereafter the Publisher emanding publication, the f of such written demand thor in writing all rights to subject to any outstanding or if permitted by the terms n any advance payments

wing royalties on by the Publisher: rdinary channels ally of 10 percent ercent of the net the net receipts

the territories or da or elsewhere ore from the list ublisher receives. rdinary channels ow), 7.5 percent ereafter. or the territories ada or elsewhere ore from the list ublisher receives. o the consumer, by the Publisher.

ns sold through amount that the

r the right, solely

the
be
for

uly
ach
and
ed
the
ake
an
ext

to
ess
hat
uct
ure

A sample publishing agreement.

they may appear. With practice, you will become very familiar and comfortable with them.

The purpose of this chapter is to give you an overview of the basic terms and conditions found in most publishing agreements. It is not meant to be a detailed analysis of publishing contracts nor does it discuss every possible variation. A complete in-depth study of publishing agreements is beyond the scope of this book. However, at the end of this chapter, I will provide you resource material where you can learn more about publishing contracts.

For the remainder of this chapter, we will go over a sample publishing agreement paragraph by paragraph.

AGREEMENT made this _____ day of _____19___, between_____, whose address is _____(hereinafter referred to as the "Author"), and _____(hereinafter referred to as the "Publisher") concerning a work tentatively titled_____ (hereinafter referred to as the "Work").

WHEREBY, in consideration of the mutual covenants herein contained, the Author and Publisher agree to the following:

The first part of the agreement simply identifies the parties involved and the work in question. It makes the statement that the following terms are agreed upon by both parties.

1. GRANT OF RIGHTS

The Author hereby grants and assigns to the Publisher and his assignee(s) and/or licensee(s) the exclusive right to publish, sell, and distribute the Work in book form, for the full term of copyright and any renewals and extensions thereof, throughout the world (hereinafter referred to as the "Territory").

This paragraph identifies the territory that you are exclusively assigning to the publisher. In this example exclusive world rights, which include all countries in all languages, are granted.

Another possible territory listing that is more restricted would be all English language rights. This would include the United States and its territories (Puerto Rico, Virgin Islands, etc.), possessions, and dependencies (Philippines), Canada, and the British Commonwealth. The British Commonwealth includes countries such as Australia, New Zealand, India, and Zambia, numbering up to 50 countries.

The contract may limit the territory to certain countries. In the United States, publishers expect at least English language rights in the U.S. and its territories, possessions, and dependencies, as well as Canada. Canada is almost always included because U.S. publishers have extensive marketing and distribution channels already set up there. Other countries may obtain rights to just their country or to all countries which speak the same language. A publisher in Portugal may buy rights to sell the book in its own country or to all Portuguese speaking countries.

In some cases, it may best for the author to give the publisher world rights and let him handle the licensing of foreign rights. However, either the author or agent may be able to make a better deal directly with foreign publishers and may retain some of these rights. For example, if a book is a biography of the former British Prime Minister Winston Churchill, the agent may retain British Commonwealth rights. He would then be free to sell these rights to a British publisher.

2. THE MANUSCRIPT

(a) The Author agrees to deliver to the Publisher not later than_____, two typewritten or computer generated copies of the complete manuscript of the Work in the English language, approximately _____ words in length, in content and form satisfactory to the Publisher. If the manuscript of the Work is not satisfactory, the Publisher may request the Author to make changes or revisions. If the Publisher requests changes and revisions, the Author shall make them within such time as the Publisher may reasonably request and resubmit the manuscript to the Publisher.

Here the delivery date and length of the completed manuscript are specified. Since many books are sold from book proposals, the manuscript is not finished on signing of the contract. The publisher allows the author the time he needs to complete it, usually giving him a little extra time since most authors run a little behind their anticipated schedules. If the author cannot meet his deadline, he needs to ask for an extension. If the work is not time-sensitive, the publisher will usually allow extra time. This request, however, needs to be made as far in advance of the due date as possible, so as to give the publisher time to make adjustments in his publishing and marketing schedules.

Another point in this clause is that the final manuscript must be in a form satisfactory to the publisher. If the publisher feels the work needs additional editing or rewriting to bring it to an acceptable form, the author is obligated to revise it. Although not specifically stated, if a work is not acceptable in its current form, the publisher is obligated to provide editorial assistance to the author.

(b) The Author shall deliver written authorizations for the use of any materials owned by a third party included in the manuscript. Any fees for such permission shall be paid by the Author.

If the author quotes a portion of a text or uses drawings or photographs from copyrighted works, he must get written permission from the copyright holder(s). Copies of the permission letters must be sent to the publisher along with the manuscript.

(c) The Author shall provide all drawings, maps, charts, photographs, and other illustrative material which Publisher deems necessary for the Work. If the Author fails to do so, the Publisher shall have the right to prepare or cause to be prepared any illustrative materials and charge the cost thereof to the Author.

In most contracts, the author is responsible for obtaining illustrations, as he is in this example. If the author fails to get suitable illustrations, the publisher is authorized to do it for him and charge the cost of doing so to the author.

(d) If, in the Publisher's opinion, an index, bibliography, foreword, introduction, or preface for the Work is necessary, the Publisher will so inform the Author. If these materials are not prepared by the Author, the Publisher shall have the right to prepare them and charge the cost therefor to the Author's account.

Material that appears in a book, either in the front or back but is not a part of the text, is referred to as front matter and back matter. Preparing this material is the author's responsibility. For some books, front matter and back matter are very important. An index, for example, is necessary for most nonfiction books. The absence of a good index will hurt the book's sales, especially among institutional buyers (schools and libraries).

(e) The Publisher shall have the right to edit the Work for the original printing and for any reprinting, provided the meaning of the text is not materially altered, and shall have the right to publish and promote the Work in suitable style as to paper, printing, binding, cover and/or jacket design, and to fix or alter title and price.

Every publishing house has its own editorial preferences and style. Each book a publisher produces will reflect this preference, as well as incorporate elements experienced editors feel will enhance the book's sales potential. If the book is reprinted or updated editions published, it may need additional editorial work.

Authors often have preconceived ideas of the form, size, price, and appearance of their books. Most authors have no concept of the factors which determine these parameters. This paragraph in the contract eliminates unreasonable requests from such authors.

(f) If the Author fails to deliver the Work within the time specified, or if the Author delivers the Work and it is not satisfactory to the Publisher, the Publisher shall have the option to terminate this Agreement; in which case, the Publisher shall not be required to publish the Work and the Author shall repay, on demand, to the Publisher any guaranteed advance or any other sums theretofore paid to the Author. Upon such termination and repayment, all rights granted to the Publisher shall revert to the Author.

If the manuscript is not delivered on time or is unacceptable to the publisher, the agreement can be canceled and any advance paid to the author must be refunded. As mentioned before, unless the work is of a timely nature, publishers are usually willing to give authors more time if they request it. Although the publisher has the right to reject manuscripts that do not meet the editor's expectations, the publisher must specify exactly why it is unacceptable and help the author correct it.

3. EDITING AND PROOFREADING
The Publisher shall furnish the Author with a galley proof of the Work. The Author agrees to read, correct, and return all proof sheets within thirty days of receipt thereof. The Author agrees to pay all charges in excess of 10 percent of the cost of composition for alterations or additions (other than corrections of printers' errors) which the Author makes in proofs, plates, or film after the type has been set in conformity with the edited manuscript returned by the Author. The cost of such changes shall be borne by the Author. If the Author fails to return the proof within the time specified above, the Publisher may publish the Work without the Author's approval of the proof.

After the manuscript has been accepted and edited, galley proofs will be made and sent to the author for review and approval. Editing corrects errors and improves the work. Occasionally, typographical or editing errors will be found in the galley. The author notes necessary changes in the galley and returns the proofs to the publisher. The publisher pays for the cost of these changes. At this stage, the work has already been typeset and corrected pages must be retyped. Sometimes the author will feel the urge to polish the work further, making enough changes in the galley to significantly increase typesetting costs. If the author's changes cost more than ten percent of the total cost of typesetting, the author will be charged this additional amount. Typsetting cost for a typical book is about $2,000 to $3,000, so the author can be charged for typesetting corrections over $200 to $300. Extensive corrections in the galley can amount to several hundred dollars. The amount charged for typesetting will vary from publisher to publisher. Ten percent, as indicated in this case, is generous. Some publishers require authors to pay for all typesetting charges over only one or two percent.

4. COMPETING WORK
     (a) The Author agrees that the Work shall be the Author's next book, and that the Author shall not undertake to write another book for another publisher until a complete manuscript for the Work has been delivered to the Publisher.

Professional writers frequently write more than one book at a time. This paragraph attempts to prevent a writer from committing to a second contract with another publisher before completing the first book. The problem with having two books under contract is that the author will end up splitting his time and energy between the two, thus causing him to delay finishing the work. This provision does not restrict the author from working on a second book at the same time, but does prevent him from committing to another contract until the first manuscript is finished.

     (b) During the term hereof, the Author shall not print or publish, or cause to be printed or published, any portion of this Work, or any other Work on the same or similar subject matter that might compete with or reduce the sales of the Work covered by this Agreement.

The publisher expects the author not to write a similar book for another publisher, which would dilute the sales of the first book. The term of the contract is for as long as the book remains in print. This does not prevent the author from writing additional books on a related subject, but they should be distinctly different. A book on baseball's greatest players and another on baseball's greatest pitchers may be too similar. Too much material would overlap. But books on baseball's early heroes, baseball's All-Stars of the 1990s, or true baseball stories, probably would not compete with each other.

5. PUBLICATION
   The Publisher agrees to publish the Work, within 24 months of the acceptance date of this contract, at its own expense; if the manufacture of the Work is delayed by the Author, by fire or water damage, material shortages, delays by suppliers or any other causes beyond the control of the Publisher, the Publisher may cancel this contract or delay publication as the Publisher deems necessary. If the Publisher fails to publish, or cause to be published, the Work within the period provided herein, and if at any time thereafter the Publisher receives written notice from the Author demanding publication, the Publisher shall within 90 days of its receipt of such written demand either publish the Work or revert to the Author in writing all rights to the Work granted to the Publisher herein (subject to any outstanding licenses which shall be assigned to the Author if permitted by the terms of such licenses) and the Author shall retain any advance payments made hereunder prior to such reversion as liquidated damages for the Publisher's failure to publish the Work.

   This clause specifies that the publisher must publish the work within a specific time frame. If it is not, then the author can cancel the contract and regain the rights which were granted. The time frame varies from publisher to publisher and in some cases from book to book, more time being given to large or complicated books. The time limit is important to the author. Without this provision, the publisher would be free to delay publication for his own interests. For example, a book might be replaced by a later one that is more timely or has greater sales potential, or it might be delayed if the publisher feels that his publication list needs to be reduced.

6. AUTHOR'S COPIES

The Publisher shall give to the Author 10 free copies of each edition of the Work published by the Publisher. The Author shall be permitted to purchase additional copies at a discount of 40 percent from the Publisher's invoice price for the Author's own use, but not for resale. Royalties shall be paid to the Author on these Author's copies.

Publishers will give the authors some free copies on publication of the work. If the author wants additional copies, he can purchase them at a discount of 40 to 50 percent. Typically, if the discount is 40 percent, the author will also be paid royalties on the author's copies. If the discount is larger, royalties are usually not paid. These copies are for the author's personal use only and are not to be resold to markets serviced by the publisher.

7. ADVANCE ROYALTIES

The Publisher shall pay to the Author, as an advance against all royalties and other payments to be earned as royalties, the sum of $5,000, payable as follows: $2,500 on receipt of a signed contract and $2,500 on delivery of an acceptable manuscript.

The advance is a portion of the royalties paid to the author before the book has earned them. The size of the advance is generally equal to the estimated total amount of royalties the book will make during the first year. The estimate is purely an educated guess because no one can accurately predict how well a book will sell. Some books that have high potential become financial failures, while others with less obvious appeal become surprising bestsellers. The more faith a publisher has in a book, the higher the advance. Huge advances—the ones you read about in the news—come from a relatively small number of the publishing giants. Large companies have more money to spend and are usually more willing to pay the largest advances. However, a medium-sized company may offer an advance larger than bigger companies because they are more enthusiastic about a book. A book with a projected list price of $10 and first year sales of 5,000 copies would yield an advance of $5,000. This would be the maximum amount the publisher would offer. For most books, first printings are limited to 5 or 10 thousand copies. Books by popular authors or celebrities would guarantee greater sales and consequently justify larger initial printings and larger advances. The great majority of advances are less than $10,000. Only five percent or less of the advances ever go over $30,000.

Advances can be paid in one lump sum or in segments. Most advances, especially the larger ones, are paid in two or even three installments. Usually payments are made on signing of the contract and on delivery of an acceptable manuscript. If the contract breaks the payments into thirds, the final payment will be made when the book is published.

8. AUTHOR'S ROYALTIES
     The Publisher shall pay to the Author the following royalties on sales, less returns, of copies of the Work published by the Publisher:
     (a) For hardcover trade editions sold through ordinary channels in the United States, except as provided below, a royalty of 10 percent of the net receipts on the first 5,000 copies; 12.5 percent of the net receipts on the next 5,000 copies; and 15 percent of the net receipts on all copies thereafter.

In most contracts, royalties increase with the number of books sold. Ten percent for the first 5,000, 12.5 percent for the next 5,000, and 15 percent for all sales over the initial 10,000 is typical. But, the percentage or the number of sales required for each increase may vary. Some contracts may give eight percent royalty on the first 5,000 copies or 10 percent on the first 10,000. If the author has some bargaining power, he may get a higher royalty or escalating steps of 3,000 copies rather than 5,000. In this example, royalties are paid on "net receipts", which means on the money that the publisher actually receives as opposed to "list price." Publishers sell the great majority of their books to dealers for resale; they must therefore sell the books at a discount from the list price. Discounts can vary from 20 to 60 percent or more, depending on quantity and purchaser. If a book has a retail list price of $10 and sells at a 40 percent discount, an author with a 10 percent royalty would receive $0.60 per book. For the same book, if the author had a 10 percent royalty based on the retail price, he would receive $1 per book—a significant and important difference. Most publishers pay on net receipts. Contracts which pay on the list price usually begin with a royalty of six or seven percent, so that the amount the author earns is fairly comparable to those paying on net receipts.

(b) On all hardcover copies sold in or for the territories or possessions of the United States, for export to Canada or elsewhere throughout the world at discounts of 50 percent or more from the list price, a royalty of 10 percent of the amount that the Publisher receives.

Books sold through normal retail channels, such as bookstores, usually receive discounts ranging from 40 to 50 percent. Special sales to nonbookstore accounts and foreign dealers often require even larger discounts. Such sales generally require more effort and more expense, and therefore generate less revenue than normal retail channels. This provision allows publishers to pursue these sales and still make a profit for themselves and their authors.

(c) For trade paperback editions sold through ordinary channels in the United States (except as otherwise provided below), 7.5 percent of net receipts up to 20,000 copies; 10 percent thereafter.

Trade paperback refers to books ordinarily sold in bookstores and does not include the smaller mass market paperbacks which are typically sold at newsstands and supermarkets. Trade paperback royalties are less than hardcover and usually more flexible. Royalties start out as low as five percent and rarely go over 10 percent. Increases come after 15,000 to 30,000 or so copies have sold.

(d) On all trade paperback copies sold in or for the territories or possessions of the United States, for export to Canada or elsewhere throughout the world at discounts of 50 percent or more from the list price, a royalty of 7.5 percent of the amount that the Publisher receives.

(e) On all copies sold directly by the Publisher to the consumer, such as by mail order or in response to ads sponsored by the Publisher, five percent of net receipts.

(f) On all copies of any of the Publisher's editions sold through remainder sales, a royalty of 10 percent of the amount that the Publisher receives in excess of manufacturing cost.

Clause (d) is similar to (b) for hardcover books, but the royalty is lower.

When a publisher sells books one or two at a time directly to the customer, greater expense is involved. To help offset fulfillment costs, clause (e) allows the publisher to pay a lower royalty. However, the royalty is based on the full retail price and not a discounted price. Most publishers give five percent.

If the book does not sell well and the publisher decides to let it go out of print, or if the paperback edition is due out soon while significant quantities of the hardcover edition are still in stock, the book may be "remaindered". To remainder a book is to sell it at a discount that is a fraction of its list price. These sales are an effort to recoup some of the printing costs. Often, the publisher will take a loss. Clause (f) allows the publisher to recover as much manufacturing costs as possible and still share any excess with the author.

9. SUBSIDIARY RIGHTS

(a) The Author grants and assigns to the Publisher the right, solely and exclusively, to exercise, to dispose of or to license the disposition of the following subsidiary rights, and shall receive 50 percent of the proceeds thereof:

1. Publication of parts of the Work in periodicals before publication in book form;
2. Publication of parts of the Work in periodicals following book publication;
3. Publication in foreign languages by other publishers (including the right to sublicense the other rights granted herein to foreign language publishers);
4. Publication in English by British or other foreign publishers (including the right to sublicense the other rights granted herein to English-language publishers);
5. Reprints in hardcover, trade paperback, or mass market editions;
6. Motion picture, dramatic, radio, and television rights;
7. Non-dramatic audio and/or visual adaptations of the Work or portions of the Work by whatever means made or transmitted, whether now in existence or hereafter invented, including but not limited to: microfilm, microfiche, information storage and retrieval systems, filmstrips, cassette tapes, and electronic transmission;
8. Book club rights;
9. Merchandising rights.

Clause (a) lists most of the subsidiary rights commonly found in trade book contracts. Some contracts separate each right differently and may attach a separate royalty to each one, others lump them together as simply, "all subsidiary rights." Agents generally prefer to retain first serial rights, British Commonwealth rights, foreign translation rights, and performance rights if the book has any sales potential in these areas. The performance rights for a how-to book on plumbing would be of little value. However, it would be important to keep performance rights, to a biography of Napoleon Bonaparte, as it could easily be adapted to the stage, screen, or television.

Publishers have subrights departments that market appropriate rights. Agents are no more capable of selling subsidiary rights than publishers, but frequently they are more enthusiastic and thus more motivated to make the best sale possible. Revenue earned from the sale of subsidiary rights can be used by the publisher to offset an unearned advance, which means that if the book does not sell well enough to earn the entire advance given to the author (which is the majority of first run books), the publisher can deduct the difference from other sources. If the agent handles the sale of these rights, the author receives all the revenue he is entitled to from these sources, as well as keeping the advance given by the original publisher. The main reason agents try to keep these rights is to prevent the publisher from retaining revenue to compensate for an unearned advance. Some books have a great deal of value in the subsidiary market, while others may not. Depending on the book, a publisher may be determined to retain subsidiary rights.

Provisions 1 and 2 refer to first and second serial rights. A magazine or newspaper that buys first serial rights is given the right to be the first to publish a particular literary work; in this case, excerpts from a book. First serial rights can be sold only once. Second serial rights are sold for excerpts printed after the book is published, or after they have appeared in another periodical. Second serial rights can be resold any number of times. Whether the work has been published once or many times, these rights are always referred to as second serial rights.

If the author has a track record of getting published, it may be to his advantage to retain serial rights as he will probably be better able to capitalize on them. Serial rights are important to the publisher because selling excerpts to popular magazines and newspapers can generate significant interest in the book and increase sales. If the author is unaccustomed to magazine article writing, it may be better to have the publisher handle serial rights.

Most publishers, as well as agents, use subagents in foreign countries to market foreign language rights. Not all books can be sold outside the country. Books which are too Americanized will not sell outside the United States. A book on the history of California would have little interest to a European publisher. Actually, very few books are able to "travel" outside the country. Publishing agreements from foreign publishers are very similar to those in the U.S., and terms are negotiable. One primary difference is the smaller size of the advance. Most countries are less populated than the U.S. and therefore have a lower sales potential. Consequently, print runs are smaller, as are the advances.

British Commonwealth rights, as mentioned earlier, may include as many as 50 different countries. Because the language is basically the same and they share interests with Americans, books published in the United States are more frequently sold to this market than in non-English speaking countries. The total percentage of U.S. books sold to this market, however, is still small.

Some publishers specialize in producing hardcover, trade paperback, or mass market paperback books. Ideally, a book will come out first in a hardcover edition, and then as a trade or a mass market paperback later. If the original publisher specializes in paperbacks, he may seek to sell hardcover rights to another publisher and come out with both editions at virtually the same time. Or there is a slight possibility that they may sell the rights to a hardcover reprint house who will print the book in a limited quantity after the paperback has been released. Reprint sales to other publishers will bring the author another advance, but it will usually be smaller than the one from the original publisher.

Performance rights include film, stage, television, and radio. Performance rights are of little value for nonfiction books. Novels and biographies have the greatest potential, yet less than 10 percent of books whose performance rights are actively marketed will actually be sold and produced. Publishers, as well as many literary agents, work with performance subagents in the entertainment industry to sell these rights.

Non-dramatic audio and/or visual adaptations of the work include most any type of presentation of the work not covered in the other provisions of the contract. Because technology is rapidly developing new products in which books can be adapted, publishers include the statement "now in existence or hereafter invented" to account for future developments. The greatest potential here is with computer software and audio and video cassettes. As computers continue to develop and people use them more for research or entertainment, adaptations of books will increase.

Book club rights allow the publisher to sell the book to a book club. Book clubs buy books at steep discounts or join in on the initial print run, allowing the publisher to print a larger number of books at a lower cost per book (the more copies printed, the lower the cost of each book). One of the advantages of having a book accepted by a book club is that it encourages the publisher's marketing staff to keep promoting the book. With large companies that print several dozen books each season, it's easy for some books to get overlooked. Also, the publicity generated by the book club will enhance the book's sales in bookstores and other outlets.

Merchandising rights allow for the licensing of companies to produce and sell products that incorporate some aspect of the book. Walt Disney's characters, for example, are used on numerous products, from stuffed toys to T-shirts.

Another common provision not mentioned in this contract is for the licensing of Braille editions for the handicapped. Most publishers grant this right free of charge, so no revenue is generated for either the author or publisher.

(b) The Publisher agrees to secure the Author's approval for the sale of licensing of any subsidiary rights, such approval not to be unreasonably withheld. All rights not herein granted are reserved for the Author.

This clause allows the author to approve any licensing agreement the publisher attempts to make. The publisher, however, is given the right to make the final decision. Allowing the author and agent to approve any offer the publisher receives from licensing efforts lets them take part in the negotiation process.

10. ACCOUNTING

(a) The Publisher shall render to the Author or his or her duly authorized representative on or before April 30 and October 31 of each year, statements of net sales up to the preceding

December 31 and June 30 respectively and, if the earned royalties exceed the guaranteed advance royalties and the amount withheld and deducted by the Publisher pursuant to this Agreement, the Publisher shall make simultaneous settlement in cash. However, if such balance is less than $25, no accounting or payment shall be required until the next settlement period in which the balance has reached $25.

Most publishers make payments twice a year. Payments cover sales made in two six-month periods, one from from January 1 to June 30 and the other from July 1 to December 31. Virtually all contracts allow publishers at least two months to tally sales and send out statements and checks. In this contract a provision is added that, if the royalty is $25 or less, the publisher may defer payment until the next settlement period when the balance has reached that amount.

(b) In making accounting, the Publisher shall have the right to allow for a 25 percent reserve against returns. If royalties in excess of the guaranteed advance payment have been paid on copies that are thereafter returned, the Publisher shall have the right to deduct the amount of such royalties on such returned copies from any future payments under this Agreement.

One of the unique aspects of the book industry is that, if a book dealer is unable to sell a certain title after a few months or a year, he may return the book to the publisher for full credit. This means that books in bookstores are not really paid for until they are sold and leave the store. Book dealers (particularly the big chain stores, like B. Dalton and Waldenbooks) may order several thousand copies of a book, only to turn around a few months later and return the majority of them. To account for possible returns, contracts allow publishers to keep in reserve 20 or 25 percent of the amount due to the author.

11. COPYRIGHT
(a) The Publisher agrees to copyright the Work in the Author's name and to secure its rights and the Author's rights

under the U.S. Copyright Act. The Publisher is authorized, but not obligated, to take steps to secure copyrights in other countries in the Territory.

The first sentence simply states that the publisher will be responsible for registering a copyright in the author's name. The publisher may register a copyright in other countries for the author or allow this to be done by foreign publishers who purchase publication rights.

(b) If the Publisher supplies, at the Publisher's expense, any textual or illustrative material for the Work, such material may be copyrighted separately, as the Publisher shall deem appropriate.

Material which the publisher supplies at his own expense can be copyrighted by the publisher or other copyright holder. For example, if illustrations are provided by the publisher, the copyright may be registered in the artist's name, rather than the author's.

(c) If, during the existence of this Agreement, the copyright shall be infringed or a claim for unfair competition shall arise from the unauthorized use of the Work or any part thereof, but not limited to, the format thereof or the characters or situations contained therein, and if the parties proceed jointly, the expenses and recoveries, if any, shall be shared equally, and if they do not proceed jointly, either party shall have the right to prosecute such action, and such party shall bear the expenses thereof, and any recoveries shall belong to such party. If such party shall not hold the record title of the copyright, the other party hereby consents that the action be brought in his or her name. The Publisher shall not be liable to the Author for the Publisher's failure to take such legal steps.

In the case of a copyright infringement, either the author or publisher or both may take legal action. If only one party is involved in making the claim, he shall pay all expenses and receive all revenues from judgments rendered.

12. WARRANTY

(a) The Author represents and warrants that the Author is the sole owner of the Work and has full power, free of any rights of any nature whatsoever in any one who might interfere herewith, to enter into this Agreement and to grant the rights hereby conveyed to the Publisher; the Work is not in the public domain; the Work has not heretofore been published in whole or in part; the Work does not infringe upon any proprietary right at common law, or any statutory copyright, or trademark right, or any other right whatsoever; the Work contains no matter which is libelous, in violation of any right of privacy, harmful to the user or any third party so as to subject the Publisher to liability or otherwise contrary to law; all statements of fact are true or based upon reasonable research; and the Work, if biographical, is authentic. The Author shall indemnify and hold the Publisher harmless from any loss, damage, expense, recovery or judgment arising from or related to any breach or alleged breach of any of the foregoing warranties. If any claim, demand, action or proceeding is successfully defended, however, the Author's indemnity shall be limited to 50 percent of the costs and expenses (including attorney's fees) incurred by the Publisher in the defense thereof.

In this clause, the author is acknowledging that he is the creator of the work and that it has not been previously published (or if it has, only under copyright), and that it does not contain libelous or harmful information that might lead to a lawsuit. If a lawsuit does result, the author is liable for up to 50 percent of the publisher's court costs.

(b) The Author shall indemnify, defend and hold the Publisher, its subsidiaries and affiliates, and its and their respective agents, officers, directors, and employees harmless from any claims, demands, suits, actions, proceedings, or prosecutions based on facts which, if true, would constitute a breach of any of the foregoing warranties (hereinafter collectively referred to as "Claims") and any liabilities, losses, expenses (including attorney's fees), or damages in consequence thereof.

If a lawsuit is brought against the publisher as a result of violating one or more of the warranties, the author can not blame the publisher or hold the company or its officers responsible.

(c) Either party shall give prompt written notice to the other party of any Claims.

(d) No compromise or settlement of any claim, demand or suit shall be made or entered into without the prior written approval of the Publisher.

(e) In the event any suit is filed, the Publisher shall have the right to withhold payments due the Author under the terms of this Agreement as security for the Author's obligations as stated above.

Paragraph (c) states that if the publisher or the author is notified of a threatened lawsuit, he must promptly notify the other. The next paragraph stipulates that the author shall inform the publisher of any settlement or compromise before the author takes any action. The last paragraph gives the publisher the right to withhold the author's royalties until after the lawsuit is settled. The money will be applied against any costs or settlements sustained by the publisher as a result of the suit.

13. REVISIONS

If the Publisher considers it necessary, the Author agrees to revise the Work on written request of the Publisher and deliver to the Publisher an acceptable manuscript for said revised edition, at such time as the Publisher may reasonably request. The provisions of this Agreement shall apply to each revision of the Work by the Author as though that revision were the Work being published for the first time under this Agreement. Further, no initial payment shall be made in connection with such revision. Should the Author not provide a revision acceptable to the Publisher within a reasonable time, or should the Author be deceased, the Publisher may arrange for the preparation of a revised edition by parties of the Publisher's selection and charge the cost of such revision against royalties due, or that may become due, the Author, and may display in the revised Work, and in advertising, the name of the person, or persons, who revised the Work.

Frequently, the life of a successful nonfiction book can be extended by updating or revising it. If the publisher feels a revision will be financially beneficial, he will request a revision. Often, just because a book has been revised, its sales will jump. In many respects, the new edition is treated like a brand new title and given more publicity and attention than it would have as just another book on the publisher's backlist. So, it is usually to the author's advantage to prepare a new edition.

14. OPTION ON NEXT WORK

The Author grants the Publisher the option to publish the Author's next book-length work on the same terms and conditions as are set forth herein and will submit the manuscript thereof to the Publisher prior to showing it to any other publisher. The Publisher shall thereupon have sixty days to advise the Author if it is going to exercise said option and upon what terms, but shall not be required to exercise it within six months following the first publication of the Work. If the Publisher does not exercise its option, or if the parties do not agree upon the terms within thirty days after the Publisher has so notified the Author, the Author shall be free to submit said work elsewhere, provided, however, that prior to the Author's making a contract with respect to such new work with another publisher, the financial terms thereof shall be submitted to the Publisher who shall have thirty days to notify the Author that it will publish the said new work on those terms.

The option clause requires the author to submit his next book to the publisher before approaching any other publishers. If the publisher does not accept the work for publication or can't agree to terms with the author, it can be submitted to other publishers. But before the author signs an agreement, he must inform the first publisher of the terms and allow him to match those terms. Some options request only the author's next book; others may require the next two or three books. The best option for the author is no option at all, but if that isn't possible, the author should option as few new books as possible.

15. TERMINATION

If the Work goes out of print in all United States editions and if the Publisher fails to reprint, or to cause a licensee to reprint, a United States edition within six months after receipt of written notice from the Author, unless prevented from doing so by circumstances beyond the Publisher's control, the Author may terminate this Agreement by written notice. Upon such termination, all rights granted hereunder, except the rights to dispose of existing stock, shall revert to the Author, subject to rights which may have been granted to third parties pursuant to this Agreement, and the Publisher shall be under no further obligations or liability to the Author except that the Author's share of earnings hereunder shall be paid when and as due. The Work shall be deemed out of print if no edition of the Work is available in the United States from the Publisher or a licensee of the Publisher and there is no license in effect which provides for the publication of an edition of the Work in the United States within 12 months after receipt of the foregoing written notice from the Author.

This provision defines what conditions constitute a book as being "out of print." It also limits the publisher from retaining the rights to a work for an indefinite amount of time. Although this clause is fair, it is not always a simple matter for the author to know when a book has been taken out of print. Publishers generally do not notify authors. The author and agent may first become aware that a book is out of print if the royalty statement lists more returns than sales. A call to the editor may provide the answer. If not, call the publisher's customer service department and ask them if the book is still available and if they have plenty in stock. When rights are given back to the author, the publisher retains some claim to rights granted to third parties (e.g., foreign publishers, film production companies, etc.) and is entitled to continue to share in revenues from them.

16. USE OF AUTHOR'S NAME

The Author grants to the Publisher the right to use, and to license others to use, the Author's name, likeness and biographical material for the purpose of advertising, publicity, and promotion of the Work.

This clause allows the publisher to use the author's biographical information and photograph on the cover of the book, in the catalog, and on flyers and other advertising materials.

17. BANKRUPTCY AND LIQUIDATION

If the Publisher is adjudicated as bankrupt or liquidates its business, this Agreement shall terminate and all rights granted to the Publisher herein shall revert to the Author automatically and without the necessity of any demand or notification.

No company is immune to financial disasters, although larger companies are considerably safer than smaller ones. Publishers are not about to advertise the fact that they are having financial problems and will conduct business as usual until the last moment, perhaps hoping things will get better. Authors and agents have no warning the publishing company they are under contract to or in negotiations with, will go bankrupt. Some publishers will continue signing contracts up to their last days. This is understandable because no author or agent will want to work with a company teetering on the brink of bankruptcy. Having agents withhold new submissions (possibly new bestsellers) could have a pronounced effect on the company's ability to overcome its financial problems.

18. MODIFICATION OR WAIVER

This Agreement constitutes the complete understanding of the Author and the Publisher with reference to the Work; there are no representations, covenants, or warranties other than those expressly set forth herein. No waiver of any term or condition of this Agreement or of any breach of this Agreement or of any part thereof, shall be deemed a waiver of any other term or condition of this Agreement or of any later breach of the Agreement or of any part thereof.

This clause limits all terms of the agreement to what is stated in the contract, but allows changes, such as the author giving the publisher additional time to publish the book, if the changes are made in writing and agreed to by both parties. Also, any breach of one part of the agreement does not invalidate the other provisions in the contract.

19. INTERPRETATION
Regardless of the place of its physical execution, this Agreement shall in all respects be interpreted, construed, and governed by the laws of the State of New York.

Publishers require that any legal problems regarding the contract be governed by the state where the publisher is located. In this example, it is New York. This makes it more difficult for an author to contest a publishing agreement and most publishers strongly resist modifying this provision.

20. CAPTION HEADINGS
Caption headings are for convenience only and are not to be deemed part of this Agreement.

Lawyers eager to prove their client's case may grasp at any technicality. This provision is an attempt to reduce such problems.

21. ASSIGNMENT
This Agreement shall be binding upon the heirs, executors, administrators, successors, or assigns of the Author, and the successors, assigns, and licensees of the Publisher, but no assignment by either party, other than an assignment by operation of law or by the Publisher to an affiliate of the Publisher, shall be made without the prior written consent of the other party.

This paragraph permits the contract to remain in force in the event that ownership of the copyright passes from the author to his or her heirs, as in the case of the author's death or disability. Similarly, if the publisher merges with another company, the contract is still binding on the new company.

22. EXECUTION AND DELIVERY OF CONTRACT

This Agreement shall be signed by the Author, or his or her agent, and returned to the Publisher within a period of two months from the date of its transmittal to the Author. The Publisher retains the right to withdraw its offer of agreement prior to delivery of the signed Agreement to the Publisher by the Author.

In this clause, the author or agent is given two months to sign and return the contract. In most cases, this is ample time. The last part of this paragraph stipulates that if the publisher changes his mind about the terms of the contract or about publishing the work, the offer can be withdrawn before receiving the signed contract.

IN WITNESS WHEREOF, the parties have signed this Agreement on the day and year written below.

Author or Author's Agent_____ Date_____

Author's Social Security Number_____ Author's Birth Date_____

Publisher_____ Date_____

Finally, the author or the agent and the publisher's representative sign and date the agreement. The publisher needs the author's social security number for income tax purposes. The birth date is required for registering the copyright.

Agency Clause

Agents without an author-agent contract will add on an agency clause stating something like the following:

All money due to the Author shall be paid to the Author's agent, _____(name & address)_____, and receipt by said agent shall be a valid discharge of such indebtedness, and said agent is hereby empowered by the Author to act on his or her behalf on all matters arising from and pertaining to the Agreement. For services rendered and to be rendered, the Author does hereby irrevocably assign to said agent a sum equal to 15 percent of all gross monies accruing to the Author with respect to this Work.

ADDITIONAL INFORMATION

This chapter covered the basic provisions found in most trade publishing agreements. To fully understand the implications of each provision and the meaning of all the terms and conditions in a contract, an entire book on the subject would be required. Fortunately, there are some good books written on this topic. Books I recommend are *How to Understand and Negotiate a Book Contract or Magazine Agreement* by Richard Balkin and *Publishing Agreements* by Charles Clark. These texts also address the differences between trade books, mass market paperbacks, children's books, religious books, and textbooks. I strongly recommend that you read and study these resources so that you have a fuller understanding of publishing agreements and the many terms and conditions contained in them.

A valuable resource that provides numerous examples of publishing contracts, including mass market and textbook contracts, is *Publishing Contracts* by Dan Poynter and Charles Kent. *Publishing Contracts* is available on disk or hardcopy only from Para Publishing, P.O. Box 4232, Santa Barbara, CA 93140. Another source of sample publishing and author-agent contracts, as well as permission letters and release forms, is *Business & Legal Forms for Authors & Self-Publishers* by Tad Crawford. Although this book is not as complete as *Publishing Contracts*, it contains informative commentary for each entry and may be found in your local library or bookstore. Other books of benefit are *Author Law & Strategies* by Brad Bunnin and Peter Beren, *Legal and Business Aspects of Book Publishing* by Richard Dannay and E. Gabriel Perle, and *Law and the Writer* by Kirk Polking. The latter book cites court findings on various court cases concerning book contracts and is a useful text for interpreting contract terminology.

NEGOTIATIONS _____

After carefully reading the previous chapter, you should have a basic understanding of publishing agreements. In this chapter, you will learn what terms can and should be negotiated. All publishing contracts favor the publisher—as you might well expect. The agent's job is to make the contract more evenly balanced.

Publishers expect agents to request changes, additions, and deletions, and for the most part are quite willing to do so. They will not hesitate to modify some terms if requested, while others they will strongly resist changing. Which terms are flexible and which are not will vary from publisher to publisher. If you have worked with a publisher before and are familiar with his policies, you will know which terms can and cannot be negotiated successfully. If you are dealing with a publishing house you have not worked with before, you will have to proceed carefully to see how firm they will stand on various terms. As you gain experience in contract negotiations and familiarlity with the publishing houses, your skill as a negotiator will grow.

THE NEGOTIATION PROCESS

Businesslike Attitude

In all negotiations, be courteous and businesslike. If you face stiff resistance on some terms, it is wise to back off and work on those the publisher is willing to modify. Publishers respect an agent who can drive a hard bargain, but will resent those who are too pushy or demanding. Your approach should be polite and somewhat low-key, not tactless or brash like a used car salesman. However, this doesn't mean that you shouldn't be persistent on terms of importance to you. The key here is to deal—be willing to make compromises. You may get a concession if you make one in return. For example, you may accept a lower advance than you would like, but in turn, request a higher royalty rate, or vice versa. You should be willing to give in on provisions the publisher firmly resists changing and, as a consolation, work on other provisions of importance to you which the publisher may be more willing to modify. This way, both sides will come away from the bargaining table feeling satisfied.

Priority List

Before discussing terms and before negotiations start, the first thing you need to do is make a list of the most important elements of the contract—the ones you are least likely to compromise. This may include the size of the advance, retaining certain rights, royalty rate, etc. Make a second list of terms you will try to get, but will be willing to sacrifice if need be. For example, modifying the option clause, publication date, etc. You may have to concede some of the items on your second list in order to convince the publisher to accept terms on your first list.

A primary point you must take into account in negotiation is the strength of your position. If the book you are selling is from a renowned author or famous celebrity, has appeal to a large mass of people, and has drawn interest from other publishers, you will be bargaining from a very strong position. You can command the best terms for your author without jeopardizing the deal. On the other hand, if you represent a first-time author or the book is projected to have only modest success and no other publisher has shown an interest, you are in a weak position for bargaining and may not be able to get much more than what the editor has offered on the company's boilerplate or standard contract. Standing firm may lose the deal. Don't be afraid to ask for changes or modifications, but be prepared to encounter firm resistance.

Frequently, editors will be willing to change some terms even if you are bargaining from a relatively weak position. The editor has already devoted much energy convincing superiors to accept the book and convinced them that the book will be of benefit to the company. Because the editor has an interest in the book, she will be willing to modify some terms if you ask. Often, the editor will offer an advance slightly less than she is actually authorized to go. So a counter offer will more than likely be met by a compromise. If not, back off and work on other terms.

Making the Deal

Negotiations begin when the editor contacts the agent and makes an initial offer. The editor may contact you either by letter or by phone, but usually the latter. This is when you start to discuss the terms of the contract. She will tell you the advance and may also give royalty rate, territory wanted, subsidiary rights, etc. Before you do anything else, you need to ask her how she feels about the book, size of the audience, tentative size of the first printing, list price, first year's sales projection, and the subsidiary rights possibilities. You need to know these parameters so that you will have an idea of how enthusiastic the publisher is and how far you can push your negotiations. With this information, you can figure an approximate range for the advance. The editor may be willing to offer as much as $15,000, but make an initial offer of only $10,000. If you have a ballpark idea of what they can offer, based on the answers to your questions, you can counter with $18,000, rather than $14,000, and end up in a better position.

You may discuss some of the more general terms on your list of priorities, but hold off on discussing the advance any further until you have had time to think about it and perhaps discuss it with the author. The editor may agree with some of your requests, reject others, and need to consult with superiors about others. She will need time to check on some requests and you will need time to consider the offer and terms agreed to thus far. This will also give you time to consider the estimated size of the advance and readjust your list of priorities if necessary. You tell the editor you need to think about the offer and inform the author of the initial terms, and that you will call her back in a day or two.

If you are unfamiliar with the publisher's boilerplate contract, you may want to request that she send you a blank copy. You can then examine it at your leisure and make notes of changes you want made before you finalize a deal.

In your next conversation with the editor, outline your requests or changes you want made to the contract and to the initial offer. If you are not sure about something, don't feel obligated to agree with the editor over the phone at that instant. Tell the editor you need some time to think the issue over and get back with her. This process may take several phone calls and several weeks.

Fill in the sample contract with the terms you discussed with the editor and write the changes on the contract. Make a photocopy of it and return the original. After the editor has had time to look over your suggested changes, she will call you to iron out any remaining points of disagreement.

Compromise is the name of the game. If you bend a little, she will bend a little. You both end up satisfied each got the best deal possible. Keep in mind to ask for a little more than you anticipate receiving, so you will have room to compromise and still have a chance of getting what you want.

The editor may be firm on the advance and royalty rate, especially if you are bargaining from a weak position. But you may salvage some compromise with some of the less important terms in the contract. For instance, author copies. If the author could use additional copies to sell to friends or business contacts, he may request more than the amount offered. The editor will be much more willing to give additional copies of the book, rather than increase the advance. If the author has a means to sell the books, it may be worthwile to obtain as many copies as possible. Most contracts prohibit the author from selling books to the publisher's normal markets, but sales to friends, seminar participants, and mail order buyers are usually permissible. Although selling books may not generate much additional income for the author, he could make enough to partially compensate for not getting a larger advance. Instead of 12 copies, ask for 30, 50, or 80 copies. Or ask to buy at a larger discount than stated in the contract. Often, publishers look at this as a publicity tool. The author will distribute the copies, thus advertising the book and hopefully generating more interest and consequently more sales.

Once all terms have been agreed to, the editor will draw up the final contract and send it to you for signing. Keep notes of your discussions and the changes you both have agreed to as the revised contract may take as long as a month to arrive.

When you receive the contract, read it over to make sure all the terms you both agreed to are included. Since the editor who negotiated the contract is not likely to be the one who actually types it, it is not unusual for contracts to contain mistakes, usually in the publisher's favor. This is not a preconceived plot against authors, but simply an error on the typist's or editor's part. For this reason, it is important that you keep accurate notes during your negotiations. You may even want to send a letter to the editor before receiving the contract, listing the terms for her verification. If a mistake is found in the contract, make the change in the margin and initial it. Then send it back for the editor to approve, initial, and return.

IMPORTANT TERMS TO BE NEGOTIATED

Advance

The most important term to negotiate in a publishing agreement is the advance. Before discussing the offer in any great detail, you must determine how much of an advance you feel the editor is willing to pay. This is based on the number of books in the first printing, list price, subsidiary sales, and the editor's enthusiasm for the book.

The advance is payment of royalties before the book has earned them. It is not a bonus or extra money the author earns. After the book has sold enough copies to earn the advanced amount, then the author will start to receive additional payments based on the royalty rate. Approximately 80 percent of the new books published go out of print after their first printing. Most of these books never earn their advance. In these cases, the author receives more money than the book actually earns and the publisher eats the loss. Since the large majority of new books published each year will not be successful enough to reprint, most authors will never receive more than the advance. The royalty rate is of no importance in such cases. For this reason, it is important that the author and agent strive to get as large an advance as possible. It may be to your advantage to request a lower royalty rate in order to increase the advance amount.

If the editor offers an advance of $6,000, her actual ceiling amount may be $7,000. You can counter by requesting $8,000. The obvious counter would be a compromise of $7,000, the maximum the editor was authorized to grant. Sometimes, the editor may not be willing to increase the advance by another $1,000, the typical increment. Try requesting an increase of $500 or even $250. This will be a relatively small sum for the publisher and he may be willing to up the figure by this amount if asked. Although an increase of a few hundred dollars does not sound like much, especially compared to the unusually high advances you hear about in the news, it's still more than you would have gotten without asking.

For inexperienced authors, advance amounts offered by each publisher are fairly standard, although they vary slightly from company to company. The large majority of advances are less than $10,000. For books by big name authors and celebrities, the advance offered by one company may vary greatly with that of another. Advances are calculated on the projected revenue the book will produce. This is just an estimate, and one company's estimate will differ from another's.

Royalty

The royalty rate is of secondary importance to the advance. If a book sells well, the royalty rate determines how much you and the author will receive. For trade hardcover books, the typical rate is 10 percent on the first 5,000 books sold, 12.5 percent on the next 5,000, and 15 percent on all books sold thereafter. Although this may represent the publisher's "standard terms" you can alter these figures. For example, you could request a starting royalty of 12 percent for the first 10,000 books and 15 percent thereafter. The numbers can vary as you see fit. Keep in mind that, because most new books will not sell more than a few thousand copies, the initial royalty rate will be the most important to you.

Royalties for paperback books range from 5 to 10 percent. No matter what you are offered, you could ask for a percentage or two increase, especially if you have asked for and been denied a higher advance. Even a half of a percent can amount to a significant increase. For example, for a book that sells for $14.95, the difference between a royalty of 8 and 8.5 percent is only 7.5 cents per book, but for 1,000 books that adds up to $75 and for 10,000 books it is $750. You can see that, if the book sells well, you can earn a significant amount, even with a half of a percent increase. This amount is relatively minor to publishers, but it is money you wouldn't otherwise have if you had not asked for it.

Territory

Most publishers want world rights for the books they publish in order to market the books to appropriate countries outside of the United States and Canada. Large publishing companies have foreign rights departments devoted to selling rights to international markets.

Most books do not "travel", that is to say, they do not appeal to people of different countries or cultures. For example, a book on U.S. politics would be of little interest to people in other countries. Likewise, a book about buying real estate in Great Britain would not interest Americans. Although there may be some people who would buy these types of books, there would not be enough to justify the expense of publishing such books in other countries. Many books printed in the United States are too Americanized for foreign markets.

If a book has potential to travel, the agent should seriously consider limiting the publisher's territory to North America, which is what American publishers expect if they can't have world or British Commonwealth rights. For a book that might sell well in South America, the agent may reserve these rights and market them separately, while allowing the publisher all other territories.

Although the agent may or may not be able to market a book or even do as well as the U.S. publisher at selling foreign rights, there is another reason for limiting the publisher's territory. If the U.S. publisher licenses a foreign publisher to print the book, the money received by the U.S. publisher is kept until the advance is earned. Let's say, for instance, the author receives a $6,000 advance against royalties. But suppose the publisher only sells enough books to pay for $5,000 of the advance. The author is $1,000 ahead of the book's actual earnings. However, if the publisher received a payment of $2,000 from licensing the book to a foreign publisher, he can keep this entire amount until the author's advance is earned out, if it ever is. Since most books do not earn out their advances, the author may not see any revenue from foreign sales. However, if the agent handled the foreign sale, the author would get the full $2,000 minus the agent's commission (including the subagent's commission), which usually totals 20 percent or $400 in this example. A common royalty split between publisher and author for foreign sales is 50/50. Out of the original $2,000 the author would receive at most $1,000 *if* the advance has been earned out. However, the author's share would be $1,600 if the agent negotiated the sale. So, regardless of how successful the book is, the author stands to gain more by allowing the agent to market the foreign rights.

Subsidiary Rights

Other important terms in a publishing agreement are the subsidiary rights. Agents usually prefer to keep most of these rights and market them separately. Agents are not any more capable of selling these rights than the publisher, however, they may have a bit more personal interest because they will share in the profits. While rights in a publishing company are handled by the rights department as part of their duties, they don't have a personal interest and may therefore be less motivated in exploiting the rights to their fullest.

With foreign rights, the agent can earn more by marketing the rights himself. Most books do not have the potential of earning subsidiary rights and, in those cases, it isn't worth spending time negotiating. But if the book has potential and the agent can effectively market these rights, it is usually best to keep them. The performing rights in a cookbook would be of little value. For a good novel though, they could be of great value and the agent should consider retaining these rights. If he knows how to approach production companies, he can do the work himself; if not, he can work with a subagent (script agent) who specializes in selling performance rights.

If the publisher resists giving up a subsidiary right, you may work on getting a better split, say, 55/45 or 60/40, with the author getting the biggest share. When advances are figured, subsidiary rights are usually included and the publisher may not be willing to relinquish certain rights. If he gives up an important right, he may insist on lowering the advance. You then must decide if the advance is more important than the subsidiary rights. Usually, the advance is more important. The most important subsidiary rights for an agent to keep are first serial rights, foreign language and British Commonwealth rights, and performance rights, as these are the rights agents and authors can most easily exploit. Other rights may be important for a specific type of book. If the agent is capable of taking advantage of the other rights as well as the publisher and feels it worth his time, he may try to retain some of these. Publishers are usually capable and willing to handle appropriate rights sales, but not always. It depends on the book and the publisher.

Option On Next Work

This provision, contained in most publishing agreements, gives the publisher the right to have the first chance to buy the author's next work. This clause is important because it can cause the author needless headaches. The option clause can have varying degrees of restrictions. The agent's goal should be to loosen the restrictions as much as possible. Ideally, there would be no option clause. The agent can shoot for this, but settle for some compromise agreeable to both parties.

Often, option clauses are worded so that the author must submit the completed manuscript to the publisher. Most books, particularly nonfiction, are sold from an outline and sample chapters before they are completed. Authors should not have to wait until they have completed their manuscripts before they can begin to market them. The option clause should allow the author to submit an outline and sample chapters to the publisher, rather than the full manuscript. Most publishers are willing to accept this modification.

You would also not want the second book to be accepted "on the same terms as herein stated." This would obligate the author to accept the same terms for the second book as were agreed to for the first. If the publisher is interested enough to want to publish the author's second book, he may also be interested enough to sweeten the deal if need be. This is especially true if the first book became a bestseller. In this case, the author, if not restricted by the option clause, could negotiate a better deal, either from the first publisher or another publisher. You should insist on including the provision that acceptance by the author and publisher be "on terms mutually agreeable." Therefore, the publisher must make a reasonable offer which, if not acceptable to the author, will free him to look for another publisher.

Often, a matching option clause is added. In this case, if the publisher rejects the second book and the author gets an offer from another publisher, the first publisher has the option to match it. If the second publisher is more suitable for the topic of the book or has a greater ability to market the book, the author may be stymied by the matching option. One possible variation of this clause that would give the author a little more advantage is a matching option plus 10 percent. So, if the second publisher offered a $10,000 advance, the first must offer $11,000 to have the right to publish the book.

Some contracts will state that the publisher does not have to exercise the option until the first manuscript is published. Since it may take as long as a year or more for publication, the author would have to wait this long before he could even begin marketing another book. This restriction is unfair and should be removed.

If the author is capable of producing books in more than one genre or more than one book a year, the option clause should be modified. Instead of the standard "The Author grants the Publisher the right to publish his next book-length work...", you should change it to something like "The Author grants the Publisher the right to publish his next book-length work of fiction written under his own name" or "under the pseudonym of..." or "featuring the character Rex Ridder." This allows the author to write books under a different name or about different characters without obligation to the first publisher.

Other Provisions

There are several other clauses that can be modified if the agent or author see the need. For example, the author is given, free of charge, a number of books as author's copies. This quantity, which is typically a dozen or so, can be increased. It is a minor provision that editors are usually willing to make. Authors are also given the privilege of buying additional copies at a discount (usually 40 percent). This can be negotiated up to 50 or even 60 percent. For most authors, this may not be important enough to dicker over, but if the author sells the books at lectures, seminars, or through mail order, this can become a very important point to negotiate.

Clauses which are of lesser importance in most negotiations include the headings listed and defined in the previous chapter: termination, revisions, accounting, publication, and manuscript. These can be modified if the author can profit in some way or if the publisher seems to take too much advantage, but generally these terms are not worth haggling over.

Most of the other provisions, such as copyright, warranty, use of author's name, bankruptcy and liquidation, modification or waiver, interpretation, assignment, and competing work are standard contract provisions and the publisher will strongly resist modifying them, and generally there would be little reason to.

FAIR DEAL

Authors who do not have agents are often so excited, when publishers show an interest in their works, that they are willing to accept almost any terms offered. The author, probably after numerous rejections, is naturally fearful of losing the opportunity of making the sale if he appears too demanding. But the editor expects to negotiate and is prepared to modify some terms even for first-time authors. Keep in mind that the bargaining power of a new author is weak and the publisher will likely end up with the advantage. But you should try to make the deal as fair as possible. If the author has a successful track record, he is entitled to receive at least a fair deal, if not gain some special concessions to his benefit.

So, what constitutes a fair deal? Let's look at what a fair deal would entail. The publisher would receive rights for the United States, its territories, and Canada. Other territorial rights should remain with the author. If the publisher controls British and foreign translation rights, he should be limited to no more than 25 percent of the income. If the book is suitable for adaptation to movies or television, the author should retain these rights. The publisher is limited to no more than 50 percent of subsidiary rights and no more than 10 percent of first-serial rights. The advance should be between $5,000 and $10,000. For hardcover books, royalties of 10 percent for the first 5,000 copies sold, 12.5 percent for the next 5,000, and 15 percent thereafter. For trade paperback books, royalties of no less than 6 percent on the first 10,000 copies sold and 7.5 percent thereafter. For mass-market paperback books, a royalty of at least 6 percent on the first 150,000 copies sold and 8 percent thereafter. Modification of the options clause to stipulate sale of subsequent books on terms which are mutually agreeable.

These are the minimum terms you should strive for with all authors. Any terms less than these favor the publisher, and terms better than these are to the author's credit. Keep in mind that the experience of the author and the publisher's enthusiasm for the book will greatly influence the final outcome.

MULTIPLE OFFERS

Simultaneous Submissions

If you send out simultaneous submissions, you always face the possibility of receiving two or more offers. All too often, however, just getting a single offer is a victory for the agent and author. Of the thousands of manuscripts and book proposals sent to publishers, only a tiny fraction ever get published. A well-written, timely book may generate enough interest to provide the agent with a choice between two or more publishers. When this happens, the agent's objective is to go with the publisher who is willing to pay the largest advance and consequently is more likely to publicize the book best. You must also weigh the strengths of each company. If one is large and has a good marketing network, you may select it over a much smaller company with less advertising/marketing muscle. However, a small company that specializes, let's say, in computer books, may greatly outsell a publishing giant for whom a computer book is of minor importance. The smaller company will give the work more attention and probably have a better marketing network of computer interest.

When faced with two or more offers, the most important item to consider is the advance. If a company is willing to invest a sizable sum in an advance, it will be committed to recouping its investment with an aggressive marketing and publicity program. Such efforts will greatly boost sales, adding to the book's chances of success.

The large majority of books receive very little attention from their publishers. Most of the publicity budget is spent on a mere handful of the publisher's most promising books. A publisher's commitment to a large advance will guarantee the book will receive substantial publicity. This fact may outweigh other factors. For example, a large publishing company may offer an advance of $15,000 with a royalty of 10 percent for the first 10,000 books sold and 15 percent for all books sold thereafter. A medium-sized company may have more faith in the book and offer an advance of $20,000 but royalties of 8 percent on the first 5,000 sold, 10 percent on the next 5,000, and 12.5 percent for sales after that. The advantages of the larger company is a better royalty rate and a larger advertising budget. With the smaller company, even though the royalty rate is not as good, a larger advance will make the publisher more committed to pushing the book. The $20,000 investment means more to the smaller company, so it would more likely push the book with greater vigor than the large company would. Besides, most books do not earn their advance, so it is generally safer to go with the company who offers the largest amount up front. However, you should consider all other factors before making a final decision.

For most books, you will approach a handful of the publishers most likely to have an interest in the books and who will be able to pay the biggest advances. If you do not get a reasonable offer, send multiple submissions to the second most likely publishers. This would include both smaller companies as well as companies that may not be as strong in the book's subject area, but who would still seriously consider publishing it. Continue to send out multiple submissions and wait for responses until the book sells.

You should always inform the editors when you send a multiple submission. You might even give a date when you would like to receive a response. For example, you might say, "I am submitting this material to a few other publishers and would appreciate your response by June 15." This puts a little pressure on the editor and lets her know there may be some competition. Many editors don't like to compete for books, but if the book has relatively good sales potential, they will seriously consider it regardless of the competition. If the book is worthy of publication yet has modest sales potential, editors will be less likely to want to deal with competition. In such cases, just inform the editor that "This is a simultaneous submission" and let it go at that.

Book Auctions

If a book has the obvious potential to become a national bestseller, then many publishers will be interested in buying it. Some publishers are willing to invest a substantial amount to obtain such a book and, if they know another publisher is interested, will even raise their initial offer to get it. It is reasonable to assume that, to get the highest price possible, publishers will have to compete with each other, with the book going to the highest bidder. This was the reasoning of Scott Meredith of the Scott Meredith Literary Agency. Thirty years ago, he extended the idea of multiple submissions into a more structured format, giving a deadline and allowing publishers to bid against each other. Scott Meredith deviated from tradition and sent copies of a hot first novel to 10 publishers, and gave them a deadline for a firm bid. The publishers responded with lucrative offers and Meredith's gamble paid off. Other agencies followed suit. Thus, the "book auction" came into being.

Everybody has heard of books selling at auctions for large five- or six-figure advances. Publishers bidding against each other for the privilege of publishing a potential blockbuster can generate huge advances.

A book that has enormous potential, written by a famous author or popular celebrity with mass appeal, can be considered for a book auction. These are relatively rare, as most books do not fit the criteria. Nothing is more frustrating than to put a book up for auction and have no one bid on it. This does happen.

When an agent gets a book that has auction potential, he will send it to the most promising publishers (those who would have the most interest and can afford to pay the highest prices). A closing date is given for the auction, after which bidding is supposed to stop. Publishers are informed of offers, although they are not told by whom, and allowed to increase their bid until they have reached their maximum and all bidding stops. In some cases, the deadline may be extended if there are some interested publishers still working on offers or waiting on approval from company officials. Delaying the deadline a day or two is not uncommon.

Some publishers will make what is called a preemptive bid, an offer that comes well before the deadline and is large enough to persuade the agent and author to stop the auction and award that publisher the book. But it is offered only on condition that all bidding stop. In order to accept a preemptive bid, the offer must be as large or larger than the highest bid you expect to receive. You may accept i, or finish the auction and hope for a larger bid. If a preemptive bid is rejected, the publisher can withdraw the offer and wait out the results of the bidding with a lower bid. This is the chance the agent takes.

After the agent receives an offer, he informs the other publishers of the amount bid, without revealing which publisher made the offer. As more bids come in, he keeps interested editors informed and encourages them to increase their bids.

On the day of the deadline, the agent should call all the editors who have not yet responded to the last bid. They are given one last chance to make a final offer. The agent's focus is primarily on the advance, but he will consider royalty rate, secondary rights, and other important terms as well. Some publishers may match the advance or come within a couple of thousand dollars of it, but also give advantages on other terms to make their offer more attractive. In doing this, the agent should stick with just the most important terms of the contract and defer any discussion of secondary issues until later. The agent will consider all factors before making a final decision.

As a courtesy, after making the final decision, the agent should call all of the editors and tell them the results and who the winning bidder is. Negotiating the finer points of the publishing agreement will take place after the auction is over.

ADDITIONAL INFORMATION

Each year, the *Author's Guild Bulletin* publishes the results of several hundred contract negotiations. You can learn a great deal about the terms agents are getting and from which publishers. This is valuable information in understanding how far publishers will go in their negotiations. The bulletin is available only to members of the Author's Guild, so you might consider joining.

In addition to the references cited in the last chapter, there are a number of other books that would be of benefit to you in understanding publishing agreements and negotiating contracts. Two of the best books on the subject are *A Writer's Guide to Contract Negotiations* by Richard Balkin and *Negotiating a Book Contract* by Mark L. Levine. They go into much more detail than most other sources on the subject. The Law Journal Seminars-Press sponsors an annual seminar on negotiating contracts. These seminars cover contracts for books, as well as television, film, and theater. For those who can't attend the seminars, audio cassettes and lecture notes are available, as well as a newsletter. For more information contact Law Journal Seminars-Press, 111 Eighth Avenue, New York, NY 10011.

RESOURCES

DIRECTORIES

Listed below are the major trade directories useful to agents. Few of them can be found in your local bookstore. Many will be in any good-sized library. If you can't find one in your area, you can write to the publisher to obtain a copy.

North American Directories

The Book Trade in Canada/L'Industrie du Livre au Canada, Ampersand Communications Services, Inc., 5606 Scobie Crescent, Monotick, ON, K4M 1B7 Canada

Canadian Publishers Directory, Quill & Quire, 70 The Esplanade, 4th Fl., Toronto ON, M5E 1R2 Canada

Canadian Writer's Guide, Fitzhenry & Whiteside, 195 Allstate Parkway, Markhaml, ON, L3R 4T8 Canada

Canadian Writer's Market, McClelland & Stewart, 481 University Ave., Suite 900, Toronto, ON, M4P 2C4 Canada

Children's Media Market Place, Neal-Schuman Publishers, 100 Varick St., New York, NY 10013

Children's Writers & Illustrators Market, Writer's Digest Books, 1507 Dana Avenue, Cincinnati, OH 45207

Christian Writer's Market Guide, Joy Publishing, P.O. Box 827, San Juan Capistrano, CA 92675

Encyclopedia of Associations, Gale Research, 835 Penobscot Bldg., Detroit, MI 48226-4094

Guide to Literary Agents and Art/Photo Reps, Writer's Digest Books, 1507 Dana Avenue, Cincinnati, OH 45207

Humor & Cartoon Markets, Writer's Digest Books, 1507 Dana Avenue, Cincinnati, OH 45207

Insider's Guide to Book Editors, Publishers, and Literary Agents, by Jeff Herman, Prima Publishing and Communications, P.O. Box 1260, Rocklin, CA 95677

Literary Agents of North America: The Complete Guide to U.S. and Canadian Literary Agencies, Author Aid Associates, 340 E. 52nd St., New York, NY 10022

Literary Market Place, R.R. Bowker, 121 Chanlon Road, New Providence, NJ 07974

Market Guide for Young Writers, Writer's Digest Books, 1507 Dana Avenue, Cincinnati, OH 45207

Mystery Writer's Market Place and Sourcebook, Writer's Digest Books, 1507 Dana Avenue, Cincinnati, OH 45207

Northwest Publishing MarketPlace, Writer's Connection, 275 Saratoga Ave., Suite 103, Santa Clara, CA 95050

Novel and Short Story Writer's Market, Writer's Digest Books, 1507 Dana Avenue, Cincinnati, OH 45207

The Playwright's Companion: A Practical Guide to Script Opportunities in the USA, Feedback Theatrebooks, 305 Madison Ave #1146, New York, NY 10165

Religious Writer's Marketplace, Running Press, 125 S. 22nd St., Philadelphia, PA 19103

Scriptwriters Market, Script Writers-Filmmakers Publishing, 8033 Sunset Blvd., Suite 306, Hollywood, CA 90046

Southwest Publishing Marketplace, Writer's Connection, 275 Saratoga Ave., Suite 103, Santa Clara, CA 95050

Travel Writer's Markets, Harvard Common Press, 535 Albany Street, Boston, MA 02118

The Writer's Handbook, The Writer, 120 Boylston Street, Boston, MA 02116

Writer's Market, Writer's Digest Books, 1507 Dana Avenue, Cincinnati, OH 45207

Writer's Northwest Handbook, Media Weavers, 1738 NE 24 St. Portland, OR 97212

Writing for the Ethnic Markets, Writer's Connection, 275 Saratoga Ave., Suite 103, Santa Clara, CA 95050

Yellow Pages, Freelance Editorial Association, P.O. Box 380835, Cambridge, MA 02238

British, Australian, and International Directories

Australian and New Zealand Booksellers and Publishers, D.W. Thorpe, 18 Salmon Street, Port Melbourne, Victoria 3207, Australia

Directory of Book Publishers, Distributors, and Wholesalers, Booksellers Association of Great Britain and Ireland, 272 Vauxhall Bridge Road, London SW1 1BA, UK

Directory of Book Publishing (2 Vols.), Oryx Press, 4041 N. Central, Phoenix, AZ 85012, USA

The European Book World, Anderson Rand Ltd., The Scotts Bindery, Russell Ct., Cambridge CB2 1HL, UK

International Authors and Writers Who's Who, Melrose Press Ltd., 3 Regal Lane, Soham, Ely, Cambridgeshire CB7 5BA, UK

International Directory of Little Magazines and Small Presses, Dustbooks, P.O. Box 100, Paradise, CA 95967, USA

International Literary Market Place, R.R. Bowker, 121 Chanlon Road, New Providence, NJ 07974, USA

Writers' & Artists' Yearbook, A&C Black Ltd., 35 Bedford Row, London WC1R 4JH England (distributed in the U.S. by Writer's Digest Books)

Writers and Photographers Marketing Guide: Directory of Australian and New Zealand Literary and Photo Markets, Australian Writers and Professional Service, Stott House, 140 Flinders Street, Melbourne, Victoria 3000, Australia

WRITER'S ORGANIZATIONS

This is a partial list of the major national and international writer's organizations in North America. For a more complete listing, including many regional organizations, see *Literary Market Place*. For a detailed listing of organizations outside North America, see *International Literary Market Place* or *The European Book World*.

Authors Guild, 330 W. 42nd Street, New York, NY 10036

Canadian Authors Association, 275 Slater Street, Suite 500, Ottawa, ON, K1P 5H9 Canada

Christian Writers Guild, 260 Fern Lane, Hume, CA 93628

International Association of Crime Writers, Inc. (North America Branch), JAF Box 1500, New York, NY 10116

The International Woman's Writing Guild, Box 810, Gracie Sta., New York, NY 10028

Mystery Writers of America, 17 E. 47th Street, 6th Fl, New York, NY 10017

The National Writers Club, Inc., 1450 S. Havana, Suite 424, Aurora, CO 80012

National Writers Union, 873 Broadway, Suite 203, New York, NY 10003

Outdoor Writers Association of America, 2017 Cato Ave., Suite 101, State College, PA 16801

PEN American Center, 568 Broadway, New York, NY 10012

Periodical Writers' Association of Canada, 54 Wolseley St., Toronto, ON M5T 1A5 Canada

Romance Writers of America, 13700 Veterans Memorial Dr., Suite 315, Houston TX 77014

Science Fiction-Fantasy Writers of America, Inc., 5 Winding Brook Dr., Suite 1B, Guilderland, NY 12084

Society of American Travel Writers, 1155 Connecticut Ave. NW, Suite 500, Washington DC 20036

Society of Children's Book Writers, 22736 Vanowen St., Suite 106, West Hills, CA 91307

Writers Connection, P.O. Box 24770, San Jose, CA 95154

Writers Guild of America (East), 555 W. 57th Street, New York, NY 10019

Writers Guild of America (West), 8955 Beverly Blvd., West Hollywood, CA 90048

Writers' Union of Canada, 24 Ryerson Ave., Toronto, ON, M5T 2P3 Canada

WRITER'S MAGAZINES

This is a list of some of the major writer's magazines in North America. Write to them for additional information about content, subscriptions, and advertising. See *International Literary Market Place* and *The European Book World* for detailed listings of magazines published outside North America.

Byline, P.O. Box 130596, Edmond OK 73013

Canadian Author & Bookman, 121 Avenue Rd., Suite 104, Toronto, ON, M5R 2G3 Canada

Freelance Writer's Report, CNW Publishing, Maple Ridge Road, North Sandwich NH 03259

New Writer's Magazine, P.O. Box 5976, Sarasota, FL 34277

Scavenger's Newsletter, 519 Ellinwood, Osage City, KS 66523

Science Fiction Chronicle, P.O. Box 22730, Brooklyn, NY 11202

The Writer, 120 Boylston St., Boston MA 02116

Writer's Digest, 1507 Dana Ave., Cincinnati, OH 45207

Writer's Guidelines, P.O. Box 608, Pittsburg, MO 65724

Writer's Journal, 3585 N. Lexington Ave., Suite 328, Arden Hills, MN 55126

Writer's Lifeline, Box 32, Cornwall, ON, K6H 5R9, Canada

The Writer's Nook News, 38114 3rd St. #181, Willoughby, OH 44094

Writer's NW, 24450 NW Hansen Rd., Hillsboro, OR 97124

Writers Connection, P.O. Box 24770, San Jose, CA 95154

BOOKS

The books listed here can provide you with a wealth of useful information about operating a successful business, understanding contracts, how to get published, learning how to work with authors and publishers, and selling scripts.

Business

Building a Profitable Business: The Proven, Step-by-Step Guide to Starting and Running Your Own Business, by Charles Chickadel and Greg Straughn (Meridian)

Help for Your Growing Homebased Business, by Barbara Brabec (Barbara Brabec Productions)

Homemade Money, by Barbara Brabec (Betterway Books)

Office At Home, by Robert Scott (Scribner's)

Small-Time Operator, by Bernard Kamoroff (Bell Springs Publishing)

Working From Home: Everything You Need to Know About Living and Working Under the Same Roof, by Paul & Sarah Edwards (Houghton Mifflin)

Contracts and Legal Issues

Author Law & Strategies, by Brad Bunnin and Peter Beren (Nolo Press)

Business & Legal Forms for Authors & Self-Publishers, by Tad Crawford (Allworth Press)

How to Understand and Negotiate a Book Contract or Magazine Agreement, by Richard Balkin (Writer's Digest Books)

Law and the Writer, by Kirk Polking (Writer's Digest Books)

The Law (in Plain English) for Writers, by Leonard D. DuBoff (Wiley)

Negotiating a Book Contract: A Guide for Authors, Agents and Lawyers, by Mark L. Levine (Moyer Bell)

Publishing Agreements: A Book of Precedents, edited by Charles Clark (New Amsterdam Books)

A Writer's Guide to Contract Negotiations, by Richard Balkin (Writer's Digest Books)

The Writer's Legal Companion, by Brad Bunnin and Peter Beren (Addison-Wesley)

Getting Published

The Awful Truth About Publishing: Why They Always Reject Your Manuscript—and What You Can Do About It, by John Boswell (Warner Books)

From Pen to Print: The Secret of Getting Published Successfully, by Ellen Kozar (Holt and Co.)

How to Get Your Book Published, by Herbert W. Bell (Writer's Digest Books)

How to Sell What You Write, by Jane Adams (G.P. Putnam's Sons)

How to Write a Book Proposal, by Michael Larsen (Writer's Digest Books)

How to Write and Sell Your First Nonfiction Book, by Oscar Collier and Frances Leighton (St. Martin's Press)

How to Write Irresistible Query Letters, by Lisa Collier Cool (Writer's Digest Books)

Manuscript Submission, by Scott Edelstein (Writer's Digest Books)

Query Letters, Cover Letters: How They Sell Your Writing, by Gordon Burgett (Communications Unlimited)

Write the Perfect Book Proposal: 10 Proposals That Sold and Why, by Jeff Herman and Deborah Adams (Wiley)

The Writer's Digest Guide to Manuscript Formats, by Dian Buchman & Seli Groves (Writer's Digest Books)

Writer's Guide to Query Letters & Cover Letters, by Gordon Burgett (Prima Publishing)

Literary Agents

Beyond the Bestseller: A Literary Agent Takes You Inside the Book Business, by Richard Curtis (New American Library)

Literary Agents: How to Get and Work with the Right One for You, by Michael Larsen (Writer's Digest Books)

Literary Agents: A Writer's Guide, by Adam Begley (Viking Penguin)

Literary Agent and the Writer: A Professional Guide, by Diane Cleaver (The Writer)

The Middle Man: The Adventures of a Literary Agent, a biography by Paul R. Reynolds (William Morrow & Co.)

A Working Marriage: What Writers Should Know About Literary Agents, by Michael Larsen (Writer's Digest Books)

Script Writing

The Complete Book of Scriptwriting, by J. Michael Straczynski (Writer's Digest Books)

The Complete Guide to Standard Script Formats, by Hillis Cole and Judith H. Haag (CMC Publishing)

The Dramatists Sourcebook, edited by Gillian Richards and Linda MacColl (Theatre Communications Group)

Getting Your Script Through the Hollywood Maze: An Insider's Guide, by Linda Stuart (Acrobat)

How to Pitch and Sell Your TV Script, by David Silver (Writer's Digest Books)

How to Sell Your Screenplay: The Real Rules of Film and Television, by Carl Sautter (New Chapter)

Professional Playscript Format Guidelines and Sample, by Mollie A Meserve (Feedback Theaterbooks)

INDEX